Not Your Usual Grief Book

How to Heal While Connecting With Your Child Who Died

By Selene Negrette

Copyright

confidentiality, I have changed their names and some details of their experience. All of the personal examples of my own life have not been altered.

Illustrations: Elise Beckman

Editing: Elise Beckman and Angela Lauria

Author's photo courtesy of Elise Beckman

Dedication

To all the members of that club nobody wants to belong to —
the bereaved parent club — may what's inside this book be a
balm to your sore hearts and help your spirit take flight.

To my beloved children: Christopher whose twinkling eyes
and infectious laughter remain etched in my heart forever and
whose lessons on unconditional love opened my eyes to another
way of living; Jonathan and Elise whose unconditional love and
support have been the rock that has sustained me. I am so
grateful for the fact that our souls contracted with each other to
go through this journey called Life!

TABLE OF CONTENTS

Introduction

"To 'move on' is to put something behind you, forget about it and never look back.
To 'go on' is to forever carry it forward with you and never forget.
A bereaved parent will never move on; we simply go on."

— Unknown

The Worst Loss of All

If you are reading this, you have experienced the unimaginable: the loss of your child. You are a survivor but do not feel like one. In fact, whether your child died from an illness, an accident, a self-inflicted injury, an overdose or was murdered, you most likely feel defeated and broken. After all, your child is no longer in your life for you to hold, to touch and to love. How can you possibly pick up the pieces and go on?

A while ago — maybe months, maybe years — you had a normal life filled with the usual daily stresses of juggling your work responsibilities or being a stay-at-home parent, of trying to maintain a nurturing marital relationship while stressing over having enough money, of trying to make time for yourself and so on until the day something truly terrible happened to your family: Your precious child died. It seemed to come out of nowhere like a level 10 earthquake, affecting every single relationship and area of your life and leaving you trembling in its aftermath — a shell of the person you once were. What you became was a version of yourself that was no longer recognizable; a "you" that now feels paralyzed because of the loss of the roadmap that guided you in life; a roadmap that has become irrelevant because not only have you changed, but the entire landscape of your life has changed as well.

In addition, this new "you" is having to grapple with the fact that your children and spouse/partner have also been changed as a result of this loss, and you, who have always been the nurturer, find yourself depleted and numb, with nothing left to give. This worries you greatly. You want to make sure that your children's grief is attended to and you do not want your marriage/relationship to fall apart either.

You find yourself in a vicious cycle of crying your heart out, putting on a brave face, then shutting down, feeling angry at the world for going on as if nothing of any consequence has happened when YOUR CHILD HAS DIED! And how dare they go on... You feel numb and do not care about anything anymore. Does any of this sound familiar?

So I ask of you, what do you think the cost will be if you continue to exist like this? Well, for starters, you know that not doing anything to get out of this cycle will affect your life negatively. There is only so much sorrow and pain your heart can take before it starts eroding and affecting all areas of your life. I know that your heart will always carry the hurt of losing your child; this will never go away, but do you think it is possible for a portion of the pain to remain while the rest of it is transmuted into a gateway to help you live again? Making the decision to do something about your current state will make the biggest difference, and someday, this terrible loss you have experienced could even help others discover there is life after losing a child. It begins with your life, with picking up this book and choosing to follow the steps. I think you know that if you do nothing, your ability to be there for your children and your spouse/partner, friends and family will be deeply diminished. Even though you think you no longer care about anything anymore, I have a feeling that — deep down inside — you know that you still do care, immensely, and it is because of your loving heart that this book has found its way to YOU at this particular time. You see, I have come to believe that your child, the child who died, is the person best suited to help you in your journey and that is why he/she plays a prominent role in the steps I discuss in this book. Why do I believe this? Because this happened to me!

This book is an invitation — from your child's heart to yours — to go on a journey of healing that will take you from feeling you are in a perpetual wintery emotional state, cold, frozen, numb and with blistery winds that come out of nowhere, to the beginning of a new springtime in your life. I am convinced that just as my child worked tirelessly to impress upon me that he was around me, loving me — and in doing so, he was the catalyst for the beginning of my learning how to live again — so does your child want the same for you. This book has something not included in grief books out there: It provides you with the tools and guidance you need to keep your connection to your child alive beyond his death and teaches you how to help your children keep their connection to their brother/sister and how to navigate through your grief together with your husband/partner. That is the reason I called this book, "Not your Usual Grief Book," because it serves as a bridge from what is offered in other grief books, i.e., the concrete steps bereaved parents can take to begin to feel a little better, *and* the steps you can take to connect with the ethereal world where your child resides now; it also invites you to embrace the sense of wonder and magic that you had as a child but lost during the process of growing up. What could be more healing for a parent than to connect with the fact that their child is around and is helping them at this time? To connect with the fact that their child can even be instrumental in helping you figure out how to learn to live again? Are you up for this journey? It will be life-changing for you. I promise!

Chapter 1 – My Story

While I was writing this book, I was thinking of you. Yes, you! You are a bereaved parent and so am I. I went through what you are going through twenty-one years ago when I lost my oldest son to cancer. As a result, several years later, I became a social worker and began to provide support and guidance to other grieving parents. I wanted to give them what was not given to me. I wanted to say the right things to them, listen wholeheartedly and honor their deep knowledge of their child. And I have done that for the past seventeen years. It has taken this long for the lessons from both my personal loss and my professional experiences to crystallize so that I could create a program with specific steps to help parents like you learn to live again.

We both have lost our most precious treasure: our child. We had no idea it was going to happen, and nobody could have prepared us for what was coming our way.

For me, March 2, 1993 seemed just like any other day, but by midnight things had begun to take on a worrisome light. My oldest son Christopher — just six years old — woke up crying and complaining that his legs hurt. Something did not seem right; he did not have a fever but did not feel or look well. My husband and I decided I would stay home with the other two children and he would take him to the local emergency room to be seen. They were there for four hours, just to be sent back home with a diagnosis of, "It's probably a virus but we drew his blood, just in case." About twenty minutes after they had been home, the phone rang. It was the hospital informing us they had found cancer cells in my son's blood and that we needed to take him first thing in the morning to the Hematology/Oncology clinic. When the doctor said the words, "Your child has leukemia," at that moment, I felt as if a thunderbolt had hit me to separate my life into two distinct compartments: life before the diagnosis and life after the diagnosis. I would never be the same; my child would never be the same; my family would never be the same, even if he survived and was cured.

He went through almost three years of intensive chemotherapy and radiation sessions with the hope he would be able to reach remission and remain cancer-free. In the end, he lost his battle and we lost it alongside him. He was brave and wise in the way children can be when facing adversity. When he died, a huge chunk of my heart went with him, and I was left feeling numb, lost, unable to move because of how intense my grief was.

Nobody can possibly begin to understand what a loss like this is like, unless they have also experienced it. And I tell you something, it does not matter whether your child died from an illness, an accident, was killed or committed suicide. Regardless of how it happened, the end result is the same. You no longer have your child here, with you. After my son died, I felt extremely alone and fragile. I had lost a very big reason to live, and even though I had other children, I still found it difficult to go on with life. Well-meaning family members and friends told me I needed to get out, join support groups, do normal things, but they had no idea there cannot be any normality when one's child has died. That your life takes on a different hue, a different smell, a different sound, a different look. Everything is different, including yourself.

It is not unlike how someone would feel if they went to bed one night, only to find out a tornado had touched down right above her house in the middle of the night. She wakes up several miles away disoriented and lost because the land is different, all the landmarks she knew are gone and she has no way of knowing how to get back home. After much effort and considerable time, she finally reaches home only to discover that it has been completely destroyed. She has lost her dwelling, her sense of safety and is going to have to start over. From having had that experience of loss, she is going to feel differently about life. She will not be taking many things for granted anymore: safety and bad weather are some of them; and she will need to learn to cope with all the fears that experience has created in her.

For parents who have lost a child, the tornado happens both externally and internally. Externally, their child is no longer there, leaving a vast chasm in the family dynamics and daily life. Activities that were normal before may come to a halt as communication lines may be affected between spouses and the other children. Internally, a lot is brewing as well. I know I felt a lot of different emotions: sadness, numbness, anger, fear, guilt. I had suffered the loss of not only my child but also people I had thought to be my friends prior to the diagnosis who afterwards had acted as if the cancer were contagious. I also felt resentment toward the rest of the world for going on as if nobody cared that my most precious child had died. And little things, like the common question, "How many children do you have?", would feel like a sudden stab to the heart — a constant reminder of my loss. My heart was so heavy that it kept me pinned to the floor; I did not want to move unless I absolutely had to.

I remember saying to myself, I don't want to go on, over and over again. I knew I had to get out of myself in order to take care of my other children, but I didn't want to. That is what raw grief does to you. And it is completely understandable! The only thing I could do was to surrender myself to it. If I felt like crying, which was most of the day, I just did. I cried until no more tears were left for that day and started again the next. There is no way to squelch such sadness, such pain, and it is not helpful to do so. I realized that only after my son's death, did I allow myself to cry the tears from when he was first diagnosed. I could not cry for the pain and fear I'd felt at the time of diagnosis because I had to focus on fighting the illness and staying positive for my son; I also could not cry for the disappointments from friendships that fell by the wayside or for the lack of understanding from family or medical staff. But after he died, I found myself crying rivers for all that accumulated stuff, and it was a relief to be able to do so. It was also exhausting; an old, deep-seated fatigue coming to the surface for all the sleepless nights I'd spent filled with worry. It is unbelievable that we parents are able to survive such heartbreak. Don't you agree?

What happens with grief is that it is cyclical; so you have days when you feel okay, but then, out of the blue, what feels like a tsunami-proportioned wave of anguish hits you, and you are left floundering and paralyzed again, and this happens over and over again. I found myself picking myself up, only to go down again because the comments that people made were so unhelpful and they looked at me with such pity whenever they saw me that, in order to cope, I isolated myself. In time I was able to attend support groups and talk with other parents who had lost children, but I found that my heart was already so heavy from my own grieving that I could not stand to burden it further with the grief of others. In the end, what I found most helpful was to develop specific daily practices to transform my thoughts and feelings away from pain and toward peace. The peace I speak of came from learning that I could connect with my child even though he was gone, and this, I realized was what I truly needed most: to keep my connection to him alive even though I could no longer touch him or see him. I became open to feeling his presence around me and recognizing the signs he was leaving everywhere to let me know he was okay and he loved me.

I have to admit that due to my science background, I had a very skeptical nature, so I still am amazed I was able to open myself to the awareness of the spiritual realm as a result of my loss. I am deeply grateful I did. Had I remained closed, I never would have learned the most profound lessons about love and about life, which my son was trying to teach me, and I would not have been able to develop the practices in this book so that I could help parents like you. I found deep healing myself as I followed these practices, and I am committed to helping you find the same kind of healing I have experienced so that you can begin to live again — not like before but differently — as you learn how to nurture your connection to your child and discover the deep inner peace that comes from tuning into the unconditional, eternal love of your child through the practices in this book.

Christopher, age 4

Chapter 2 - The Program

"From Winter to Spring"

The loss of my son marked the beginning for me of a different awareness about life, of a newfound willingness to try ideas and things I would have never been open to before his illness and subsequent death. I decided to go back to school to get a Master's in Social Work so that I could help other families who were going through the same experience as me. I could say that I went from feeling like my soul was in winter to experiencing a sense of spring and renewal.

Parents such as ourselves need a program developed by someone who has been there and who is now on the other side of that grief. A program that offers us specific steps to follow, not to take away the pain or the grief, but rather to help us learn how to live again a little bit at a time and heal as we adjust to functioning in a life in which a huge chunk of our hearts is missing. I have developed an 8-step program entitled "From

Winter to Spring." Each following chapter is dedicated to one step and follows a progression from the numb and barren grief of winter to the ultimate goal of returning to the essence of life in spring. By following these steps, chapter by chapter, you are giving yourself the golden opportunity to transform your internal landscape and with it, every aspect of your life for the better. These steps, outlined below, are the same ones that helped me learn to live again after my son Christopher died, and I am confident they will be able to help you as well.

1. The Blizzard

I call it the blizzard because I feel it captures the cold, dreary, chaotic and confused mental and emotional place where us parents live after our child's death. This step encourages the use of writing catharsis letters as a way to release heavy feelings, as well as having a ritual to dispose of the letters to symbolically let go of those feelings that weigh us down, thereby creating space inside of us for light to later shine through.

> *"When I found myself in a bottomless pit of feelings, whether it be anger, sadness or guilt, I would write a letter and then burn it. This simple act brought me such relief! And it also gave me some measure of clarity as to all I was feeling so that I could be proactive and take steps to heal. This practice was transformative for me. It slowly but surely allowed me to safely release all the burdens I had been carrying for so long."*

2. Shimmering in the Snow

This step leads us to a point in which we can take control over some of the things that are not helping us on our journey. It invites us to try to be grateful for our child's life, much like noticing that even though snow is cold, there is still beauty in the way it shimmers. It invites us to become aware of the way our thoughts determine how we feel and encourages the use of affirmations to help reshape our newfound reality. It also introduces the "blessing your child" practice for us to do every time we think of our child so that we can, little by little, transform the way we feel.

> *"By paying attention to how the thoughts I was having affected how I felt, I realized that dwelling on certain memories or thoughts only brought misery for me, so I began to use positive affirmations to get me out of the temporary funk. I would also bless Christopher and thank him for being in my life, for all the wonderful things he taught me and for who he was. Dwelling on these things softened my heart and brought in a sense of gratitude for the fact that I did get to have him in my life even though it was not for as long as I would have wished. It is amazing how choosing to be grateful could transform and uplift my entire day."*

3. A Patch of Blue in the Skies

After following the previous steps, we can begin to see through the blizzard and gray skies to notice a little patch of blue just beginning to break through. This is the start of our acceptance of the profound ways in which our loss has changed who we are as a person and how we view life. In offering kindness to the new "you" as a result of that recognition, we begin to see that small patch of blue; it gives us a bit of hope.

> *"After my son's death, I felt utterly lost because nobody could understand my experience. I could not connect to others in the same way I had before. I was profoundly changed. Recognizing this helped me find different ways to cope because the old ones did not work, and it also led me to offer kindness to myself because it is not easy to have the course of your life dramatically changed against your will."*

4. Footsteps in the Snow

At the beginning of our grief process, we feel paralyzed and numb. Our grief is such a traumatic experience because we know that no parent should ever have to lose a child. In this fourth step, we begin to come out of our paralyzed state to take tentative steps toward personal healing, and this has to start with offering love to ourselves. Coming to terms with the child within us, what it needs in order to go on and finding a way to connect with it — so that we can identify how to best nurture ourselves — is much encouraged here. In this way, we leave our footprints in the snow as we make progress on our journey.

> *"One of the biggest lessons I learned was about love. While Christopher was battling leukemia, I suddenly became aware of the quality of his love for me. It was pure, selfless and unlike anything else I have ever experienced. My guess is that your child offered you that same kind of unconditional love — literally, love without conditions. To move forward, I realized I had to learn how to find my inner reservoir of unconditional love and offer it to myself. So I vowed to work for the rest of my life if necessary to become an unconditional love-giver. With this step in the process, I am inviting you to nurture yourself so that you can give love from a place of fullness, rather than a place of scarcity. When you do this, you are loving unconditionally, which is the best possible thing for you, your family and every area of your life."*

5. The Bridge

Our children and loved ones, and the love we have for them, is the force that prompts as to live again. If it weren't for them, we would stay in that same place forever where we last were with our lost child. They are the bridge that can lead us to experience spring again; not in the same way we did before our child's death, for that is not possible. It will be a different kind of spring, but nonetheless, it will bring with it hope and much-needed direction. This step guides us parents so that we can learn to identify what our children and loved ones need from us so that we can support them in their grief. It also invites us to develop memory-making rituals together to bring a sense of connection between them and the brother or sister they lost.

> *"Just as we need to say goodbye to our loved one who has died, so do our children. And just as you would benefit from keeping the connection to your child alive, so would your children. What I did with my children was to engage them in conversations about their brother in which we exchanged stories, funny, sad or touching ones, which kept Christopher present in their minds and hearts. I made a mini photo album featuring photos of each of my children with Christopher and placed it on their nightstand for them to look at when they missed their brother. I also had them pick out a toy of their brother's for them to keep and cherish. And they fully embraced these activities, which I believe did much to help them as they grieved for their older brother."*

6. Grass Underfoot

When we are grieving, our thoughts and feelings get muddled, and this can affect the quality of our relationships. Our marital/romantic relationship without doubt has been impacted by the change, but in coming to a place of more clarity by now, we can take the steps we need to find common ground again. This sixth step encourages us parents to recognize that we each grieve in our own way, and it guides us to learn to develop memory-affirming activities of the lost child that can be done together as a couple. It also encourages showing mutual respect. In taking steps to honor where each of us is in the grief continuum, we begin to feel some green grass coming through the cold snow.

> *"You and your spouse/partner have gone through a traumatic experience, and sometimes, that can break you apart; other times, it can bring you closer. No matter what, it is important to respect each other's way of grieving and do all you can to make decisions with the best interests of the children in mind, first and foremost."*

7. Wildflowers Everywhere

As we follow all the steps above, we being to feel lighter and more open to trying new things. The tools in this seventh step invite us parents to find our own way to communicate with the child we've lost so that we can nurture the bond we have with them and allow the child who died to continue to help us and soothe our sore hearts. These tools are as follows: using letters to communicate with your child who died, becoming aware of signs and symbols as messages from your child, learning to listen to your intuition, communicating with angels or divine guides who are here to dispel your fears and worries, and connecting to your sense of wonder at the magic of life. As a result of realizing there are invisible realms just waiting to help us through this very difficult time, we will begin to notice the different colors that pop up in our lives; our lives will no longer be gray. Our connection to our child will be nurtured, which will bring out the wonder we felt as children, just like the sense of awe your child felt when they came across a beautiful wildflower.

> *"Something I learned was that just because Christopher had died, it did not mean I couldn't find a way to keep my connection with him. I felt that my bond with him was forever; that my heart had an invisible string attached to his heart that could never be broken. In the end, he was the one who made sure I realized he was around me. He came to me in vivid dreams that felt like visits, I heard his footsteps on the stairs on Christmas Day, he made sure "our song" played on the radio on the way to his grave — there were so many signs... He helped me realize that just because I couldn't see him anymore, it did not mean he wasn't there with me every step of the way. Because of him, I learned to trust in my intuition and be open to messages from angels; I became in touch again with the sense of wonder and magic I once had as a child but had lost as I grew up."*

8. Monarch Butterflies

Butterflies bring color and joy to our lives. They also remind us we are on a journey of the soul and the things that happen in our lives have the potential to turn us into even better beings. They speak to us of how hard we have worked to transform ourselves. As parents, nothing could affect us more than the loss of our child, and even though we know we can grow from that heart-wrenching experience, that does not mean we want to nor truly believe we can. It is so hard to even consider the possibility of feeling joy or happiness again. Our joy may never be the innocent one we once knew; it may be tinged with bittersweetness forever, but it is definitely possible to be happy once more — I know this from personal experience. This step encourages us to use meditations I provide so we can visit our child as well as our future selves in order to co-create a plan to learn to live again.

> *"It is my firm belief that your child will lead you to the life you are meant to live and that in your connection with him or her lies the key to your healing. This is what happened to me with my son, and it is my hope that you will open yourself up to this unique and special approach to healing as you continue in your journey."*

I know there are not many grief books out there with this type of unconventional approach to healing after the death of a child, but I can tell you from personal experience that these are the authentic steps that allowed me to rediscover life after my child died. It took me a long time to heal, but I truly feel that following this 8-step guide will greatly accelerate your journey to finding spring and healing and becoming the best version of yourself for your other children, your spouse, and yourself. Furthermore, I know that it is through the guidance and support of my own son Christopher that this book has come to be written; therefore, I feel that its contents are supercharged with all the magic you need to bring this beautiful transformation to in your life. Immerse yourself in it as we dive into the program ahead!

Chapter 3 – The Blizzard

"If our thinking is negative, we can drown in a sea of negativity; if it's positive, we can float on the ocean of life."

— Louise Hay

You are now beginning the first step in the journey "From Winter to Spring" — a step which I call the "Blizzard." Why do I call it this? Because I feel it perfectly describes the inner landscape of us, the bereaved parents. Many times we feel numb and barren inside, but that is because we are so exhausted from battling the raging blizzard of our overwhelming emotions and grief that we stop feeling them. In the middle of this winter storm, we become so cold that we can no longer see or even feel at all. I know I felt that way for quite a while until eventually I learned how to help myself out of the snowstorm, but it took me a lot longer than it would have if I had had someone to guide me, someone who knew the terrain and could help lead and support me in the process. How have you been feeling and what do you think can help you at this time? You probably are thinking that nothing can help you because *the* only thing that could is to have your child back. I know. Remember, I have been there too. But we can take this step together as I show you the way out of the storm's confusion and turmoil. I'll be your guide, and I'll share the navigation tools I myself used to help me leave the blizzard behind after losing my oldest son Christopher.

My Healing Journal

As you move through the eight steps of healing, you can follow the online workbook, "My Healing Journal" at the following link:

www.notyourusualgriefbook.com/myhealingjournal

You can use your own journal and make entries based on the PDF workbook or you may choose to print out the entire online workbook and fill it out as you go — whichever works for you is completely fine. The important part is, this workbook will serve as a supplemental guide helping you follow along with the book so you can get the most out of the tools and practices I lay out in the chapters ahead. In the end you will have a "healing journal" completely your own!

When you are ready to do the exercises detailed in this chapter and the chapters to come, just go to your healing journal and begin!

Catharsis Letters

A tool I have found to be of help is writing letters right at the time you are feeling intense sadness, anger, despair, fear or guilt. Just putting all those emotions down on paper is an immensely beneficial exercise. Research has shown that when writing, people experience a sense of relaxation and stress relief that helps improve their mood level, overall health and outlook on life. Keep the healing journal on your nightstand or coffee table, ready to be used when needed. Use it in the moment, use it as you cry, write down every feeling you are experiencing until your words and tears run dry and there is nothing left to say. I promise this will help you find your way out of the blizzard, and each time, it will become a tiny bit easier. See your journal as your ally and an amazing listener. Are you willing to give this a try and see if it lessens in any way the degree of your emotional swings? Go ahead, give it a try. You have nothing to lose!

The Weekly Inventory

Another helpful tool you can use within your journaling practice is to take a weekly inventory of the feelings you have been writing about in your letters to help you identify which are most prevalent. Review all your entries from that week and underline key phrases or words you use repetitively. If you do this on a regular basis, you can begin to pick up on thought patterns that may be pushing you further down. This will help you choose new ones that help pull you up. After you have gone through the week's entries and made all your underlines, flip to a fresh page under "Weekly Inventory." Here, you will write all of those key phrases you underlined along with a summary of how you think they affect your emotional state. For example: Are you blaming yourself for your child's death? Are you angry at God? Are you recriminating your spouse? These feelings of blame, anger or recrimination may be adding weight to your grief, which is only detrimental to your well-being and healing. After narrowing it down to one predominant theme of what you have been mentally focusing on that week, your task is to think of a way that you can turn that negative statement — something like "I am furious that God took my child away" — into a positive statement that will affirm that there is something you can do about it — "I am grateful I had my child for as long as I did" might be one option. This process can guide you to the best way to help yourself through your grief by exchanging a very heavy feeling for one of hope or gratitude. You did have your child for a time, and even if gratitude for that time is not what you are most often feeling, you can begin a shift by actively choosing to dwell upon it.

As another example, I myself instinctively turned to writing letters during the first weeks and months after my son died, and sometime later when I went back to examine them, I identified my most prevalent feeling had been guilt — I had wanted to be perfect for my son at every moment, and inevitably, there were times when I felt I had failed. Later on, I connected the dots and came to realize I had been dwelling on the very few moments when I had not lived up to my standards as a mother while I had been totally disregarding the millions of times when I had given 1,000% to him. After this realization, I was able to let go of the guilt as I chose to remember and celebrate my love, commitment and dedication to my child. You see now how writing helped me realize how guilty I felt, which, in turn, led to the realization that by dwelling on the negative and ignoring the positive, I was punishing myself at a time when I was at my lowest point. I was able to change my thinking and thereafter be one step closer to real healing. That is how powerful and transformative writing and reviewing our feelings can be!

Developing Your Own Healing Rituals

The most important role of a ritual is to bring some measure of order to a life of chaos and confusion. Grief is chaos, wouldn't you agree? Therefore, when we are grieving, that is the time when we need rituals the most. Unfortunately, the death-denying society in which we live does not provide us with many rituals to help us in our grief. But we can create our own rituals to help ourselves. I have benefitted greatly, and many of my clients have as well, from adding some of the following healing rituals to our lives:

1. There comes a time when your catharsis letters feel redundant. Maybe it's been weeks of you feeling the same negative emotion, and you want to release it for good and for all. In this case, creating a symbolic ritual can greatly help you in this process. After writing a particularly burdensome catharsis letter, remove the page from your journal and fold it up. Now place this letter inside a glass jar and burn it or throw it in the fireplace. This simple ritual works at a subtle level and represents your conscious desire to let go of the feelings holding you down and to stop experiencing the same incapacitating effects that those negative emotions are having on your life at this time. I am not talking here about your feelings of sadness; I am talking about regret, fear, anger and guilt, because these are the feelings piling up on top of your sadness and making it an impossible load for you to carry. This symbolic burning is a release and can do wonders for you in the process of healing.

2. Another important ritual you can try is to write a loving note to your child, tie it to a balloon and release it to the wind as a message to him or her. You can do this with your family and loved ones later on, but start by trying

this on your own as a personal way to connect with the child you lost. This symbolic gesture is not only beautiful, but also powerful, as you are raising your eyes to the sky and focusing purely on your love for your child. Another option would be to burn the letter, as people in some cultures do, because they believe the smoke will carry their message of love to their loved ones.

3. Burning a candle every time you find yourself wishing you could speak directly with your child, especially in the early mornings or before bed, and holding a mental conversation with him or her can also be a powerful way to express and release your feelings. Next time you find yourself wishing your child were near, go to a room where you can be alone, turn off the lights and light a candle. By focusing on the gentle light of the single flame and watching its flickering movements, you will move to a more relaxed, almost meditative state. Imagine your child's face on the other side of the candle and, in your mind or out loud, say exactly what you wish to say to him or her, as if your child were really there in front of you. Trust that your child is there in spirit and that the candle is a beautiful conduit for your messages and feelings.

Feeling Different

One of the most difficult things we bereaved parents experience is the overriding sense that we no longer fit in, in the world. The activities and priorities that used to matter no longer do; the concerns and worries we used to have no longer seem to matter, and because of this, we feel so different from other people. Being around family members or friends who seem so carefree and share their normal day-to-day concerns we used to have only intensifies the despair at not being able to relate anymore. Does this resonate with you? I know I felt very alone, and I particularly felt that nobody, *absolutely nobody*, could understand how I felt or how much I had lost.

I know I found myself feeling angry and frustrated at people I cared about because of this. I remember clearly the time, a friend of mine called me and started to sob inconsolably as she shared with me that she had just been told that her five-year-old daughter needed glasses. I couldn't believe my ears and I became so angry that this person could be saying this to me when I would have given my life for that to be my problem. At the time, I had just been told that my child had only six months left to live! Her dramatic emotions over something so trivial in comparison made me resent her for being so insensitive as to bring it up with me in conversation, and I felt more distanced than ever from the concerns of the people around me!

I have come to realize with time that everybody is in their own little world and that even though people do care, they have great — and I mean *great* — difficulty putting themselves in the shoes of parents such as ourselves who are dealing with such great fears and such tremendous loss. This is the reason it is very important for you, as a bereaved parent, to have the proper tools in your belt that you can use to deal with the feelings that can arise in social situations. I have named them as follows:

1. The Expectation-Adjuster Wrench: Just like a wrench, we can use this tool to adjust our expectations of what other people are capable of before we enter a social situation. I believe doing so can help us deal with difficult circumstances. Do not expect others to understand your new reality, because unless they have experienced the same loss in their own lives, they have no idea what it is like, despite even the best intentions, and can stumble badly in what they say or avoid. Life as you knew it may have stopped for you when your child died, but for everyone else, life just goes on. Learning to accept this and letting go of the expectation they can truly understand what you are going through is a key tool and one you can use before you even meet with your friends, family members and other people outside your closest circle.

2- The Answer Pre-Calculator: Mentally prepare yourself for how you are going to answer questions that people may ask. How many children do you have is a particularly hard one, and it is best to decide what you are going to say beforehand so as to avoid feeling awkward or that you have been put on the spotlight. If you have already pre-calculated your answer, you will be able to smoothly answer in a way that does not make you feel uncomfortable.

3. The Quick-Draw Escape Saw: When you realize you have spent enough time in a social situation and wish to curtail it quickly, it is important to have a quick-draw excuse you can use to leave the situation. Something like "I have to go to another engagement" or "I'm needed at home" would work — anything you have prepared beforehand that you can pull out whenever you need to leave and cut any pleas for you to stay in half. You need to have a firmness and a finality in your tone to indicate you are committed to leaving for your own well-being and will not stick around just to please others. Having a plan B allows you to leave a gathering early when people start having "normal fun" and you find it intolerable, or when somebody makes a comment that only makes you feel worse. This is part of taking care of yourself, and this is a necessary tool for any social situation.

4. The Special Date Organizer: Prepare in advance for any especially difficult and emotionally charged dates, such as holidays, birthdays and anniversaries, as if it were to be written down in an official "organizing" binder. Include a mental picture of the date, including who you want around you on that day, where you want it to take place, and what activities will help you and your loved ones in your grief. It is important to create a complete "entry" for each special date so that you don't allow other people to come in with their own suggestions that are not rooted in what is best for *you* at this time. It may even be helpful for you to actually write these details down for yourself or to pass on that information to someone else if you wish for them to help you plan the specific day. It should be sacred and treated as such, but it can only be so if you are clear about what *you* feel is best to honor the occasion.

5. The Safety Net: Identify one or two people you can count on to be there for you when you have had a bad experience with somebody and are struggling. These people will be your safety net, the ones you can fall back on when social situations go awry, and who can help you get your thoughts and feelings back together afterwards. Make sure you can call or meet with them and that they are reliable. If there is no one you feel you can rely on as a safety net, who you feel is a good neutralizer when tough emotions pop up, then decide on a place that makes you feel safe and go there to be alone and restore yourself whenever you feel like you've been thrown off-balance by a negative situation. You can also write in your journal to let out your feelings at that time. The safety net is a very important tool to have in your belt moving forward, and it can expand to fit as few or as many people as you choose.

Here are some examples of how the application of the above-mentioned tools made a difference on some of my clients' lives:

Cathy and Edward

These parents did everything together, and accordingly, after their only child died, they planned ahead and decided that if somebody they didn't know asked them the question: "How many children do you have?" they would say none; but if it were someone they would continue to socialize with and see, then they would tell them that they had one child, but that she had died. They shared with me that this worked for them and that talking and deciding about it in advance went a long way to diminish their anxiety and distress in social situations. This a great example of how the Answer Pre-Calculator tool can truly make a difference in helping you handle difficult questions when they arise.

Katie

I remember one young mother, Katie, whose son had died four months before Christmas. Realizing that she would not be able to withstand the pain of spending Christmas at her home without her child, Katie wisely decided to go out of state and spend the whole season with her family and she shared with me that it helped her immensely. She knew that had she stayed, her grieving heart would not have been able to tolerate it and she had her young surviving child to think about and take care of. Katie used the Special Date Organizer tool by realizing that she was in control over where, how and with whom she spent the holidays, and this aided her greatly in surviving her first Christmas without her beloved child.

Chapter 4 – Shimmering in the Snow

"Nobody is exempt from the trials of life, but everyone can always find something positive in everything even in the worst of times."

— Roy T. Bennet

This step is called "Shimmering in the Snow" because when we are in the midst of the blizzard of our grief, we tend to dwell on the coldness and the horrible conditions; most likely, we are not able to notice the shimmering of the snow that coexists with the blizzard. Whether we realize it or not, our internal landscape is changing as we bereaved parents continue on our journey of grief. In this chapter, I offer some practices that can lead you to begin to notice the shimmering in the snow — the positive things that may be hidden in the midst of your grief.

Many times, the blizzard has a hold over us that can seem unending. This is completely normal. I, for one, kept reliving everything that had happened since the moment my son was diagnosed until the moment he took his last breath. This is of course understandable! How can you make peace with something as unacceptable as the loss of your child? But what this did was keep me in a cycle of sadness and darkness that I could not find a way to get out of. As time went on, as it inexorably does, the grief felt like it was getting worse, instead of better. So what can we do to help ourselves feel better? How can we begin to notice the shimmering snow during our emotional state of winter?

We Are What We Think

I am sure you have heard or seen the following phrase: "We are what we think." Do you believe this? Louise Hay talks about this in her famous book "You Can Heal Your Life." She states that "no matter what the problem is, our experiences are just outer effects of inner thoughts. You have a sad thought, and it produces a feeling. Change the thought, and the feeling must go." As a bereaved parent myself, I did not want to stop feeling the loss of my child; I realized that working with my thoughts would not take away the sadness. But I did see it could open up a little room for my sadness to lessen enough to allow me to function better in my day-to-day life. And it did help me!

Wouldn't you welcome having certain tools you can use to feel less numb, less exhausted?

As I became aware of what thoughts were going through my mind, I gained some measure of control over them so that I could change them into more positive ideas. Not that I stopped grieving, it was more so in doing those certain things, I was able to move from standing paralyzed at the entrance of the dark tunnel that was my grief, to taking a few tentative steps toward the flicker of light I could barely see a long way down. It has been twenty-one years since my son died and I am still grieving. I will grieve until I take my last breath, but the difference is that my grief no longer incapacitates me, rather it propels me to do something productive and helpful for myself and others. You can also do this. I know it!

Take a sheet of paper and write your child's name at the top. Then, write down all the recurring thoughts you have on a daily basis. Fill the sheet. After it's full, I want you to underline all the thoughts that felt like daggers when you wrote them or when you re-read them, such as "Why wasn't I a better mother to you?" Circle any thoughts that felt like a hug to your heart, such as "I love you." You probably wrote mostly thoughts that felt painful to you, and that's normal and totally okay. If there were any phrases you circled, I want you to turn the page over, write your child's name again at the top, and copy them directly onto the fresh page. These are the thoughts you need to re-route yourself to whenever you are feeling weighed down by the heavier thoughts. If you had no uplifting thoughts on the first page to circle, then your task is to turn the page over and try to fill that page up with as many thoughts and statements as you can that feel like a heart-hug to you when you read them. Focus on these thoughts throughout your day, carry this list in your pocket, learn how to notice when you are focusing on a self-defeating thought or cycle, and shift out from it into a more positive, loving thought-place, and you will truly be on your way toward beginning to notice the shimmering in the snow around you!

Blessing Your Child

I am going to share with you a very powerful practice that can support you in your commitment to move through your grief. How do I know this? Because it helped me! I did this during the darkest times of my grief when I was feeling raw and hopeless. I started blessing Christopher every time I found myself dwelling on his death, on the loss, on how much I missed holding his little "tiger paw" hands, or his twinkling green eyes or his playful and mischievous nature or his sweet voice... You get the picture: The list of things I missed about him could go on and on. What I began to do was to switch my thoughts from his diagnosis, illness and death to his life, to the light and laughter he brought to whatever he did and everyone he met. I decided to dwell on the gift that it was to have had him for almost nine years and on the many ways in which he had touched me and so many others with his courageous and loving heart. I blessed him every time I thought of him. And do you know what happened? My heart began to feel lighter, at first just a tiny bit, but in time, it started to heal and become filled with the many gifts he left me and my family with. I began to celebrate his life every time I thought of him, and that, in time, had a transformative effect on my grief and my life. I began to see the shimmering in the snow! I invite you today to try this and see for yourself if it helps you in any way.

Transferring the Blessings

You can take the "Blessing Your Child" practice further by beginning to bless the people and circumstances that were put in your path to help you during your journey with your child: those friends, family members, doctors, therapists, strangers who were good to your child and who may continue to be involved in your life. Taking the time to consciously dwell on the goodness that surrounded you and your child in the midst of the difficulties and sadness surrounding the loss of your child will transform your feeling state significantly and allow you to take another small yet powerful step forward even though you are still grieving.

Sometimes in the midst of our grief, we forget to connect to the magic present in life — the magic you were so keenly aware of on the day your child was born is still present in your life every single day, and what thoughts you choose to dwell on is the key to whether you notice that magic. I know I could not connect to it after Christopher's death because I felt so destroyed by my grief. However, I slowly began to recollect little details I had previously overlooked, little magical things that had happened to help us both along the way. I recalled that, as things were changing and Christopher's life was nearing the end, out of the blue, two of his preschool teachers drove all the way from Kentucky to Georgia on Thanksgiving Day — leaving their own families on such a holiday — to visit him and bring me a very important message: that I needed to talk with him about dying; that I needed to reassure him that he did not need to be afraid, that he would be going to a realm where he would not be sick. After their visit, I sat down and had that very difficult conversation with Christopher, and I am so grateful for the divine intervention that allowed for that to happen and for the loving messengers who followed their hearts and came to our aid at such a time of need.

Do you see how intentionally focusing on the people, circumstances and mysterious happenings that helped you during your difficult time can shift your feeling state from very low and empty to a lighter and more full state?

Those Memories...

Part of the burden we carry, as bereaved parents, is not knowing how to deal with all those memories. There are so many of them, some wonderful and loving, others funny and fun; still others, poignant and extremely sad. We are weighed down by so many memories, but cannot bear to part with them, as they are all so very precious although heartbreaking. The reason this is so hard is because we have been traumatized. The loss of a child is a deeply traumatic event!

Symbolically transferring those memories to a special box or container can help you feel a bit lighter. A helpful practice is to find or make a beautiful box for your memories; it could also be a large glass or ceramic jar that you can place in a special location in your home. Whenever you think of it, write down any of the positive, funny, special, loving memories you have with your child on strips of paper and place them in the box or jar so that when you are at your lowest and do not feel like writing a catharsis letter, for example, you can just go to the container and pick up one of the strips of paper to read about a wonderful memory of your precious child. You can also place photos of your child there. What is important is to keep it positive, touching and up-lifting so that you can help yourself out of the worse moments of your grief. It is not that you will be less sad. How can anything make you feel less sad? But what doing this will do for you is introduce small moments in time when you can dwell on the beauty, carefreeness and preciousness of your child and the qualities that made him or her so special to you and to the world at large. And in doing so, you will take another tiny step forward. Try it and see if it does indeed help you. I know it helped me at a time when I felt that life was not worth living because my heart was so devastated! I had two other young children who were counting on me to help them, but yet, I have to admit it was a daily struggle to continue living when every cell of my body did not want to. As I started paying attention to my thoughts and slowly began to redirect them, as I wrote down and later read about some of the wonderful memories I had made with my child, and as I began to bless my Christopher when I found myself dwelling on his dying, rather than on his living, I slowly began to move forward. These were baby steps, but they got me out of my paralyzed and frozen state nonetheless. Those positive thoughts, blessings and memories were the brief but beautiful moments when I noticed the shimmering of the snow. You can do this too! I have every bit of confidence in your ability and commitment to follow these suggestions to see how they can make a difference in your life now.

A Collector of Inspiring Materials

While I was going through the hardest, rawest times of my grief, I had an idea. It came out of the blue and it led me to begin

Not Your Usual Grief Book

a collection. That's right! As depleted as I felt, I took time to search for and find inspiring sayings, books, paintings and such that would lift my spirits. I was grazing the floor with my soul and knew that I desperately needed help.

I probably read every book that had been written at the time on angels and developed a beautiful connection with their presence. It felt to me as if they were trying to make their presence known to me, to let me know I was not alone in my grief and that they could help me, if only I asked. I became intensely curious and more open-minded and thought a lot about what might happen to us after we die. There is a magical thing that happens when you become a collector of inspiring materials, and that is that these things become magnetized to you and show up in the most random and beautiful of places. Inspiring quotes, books, etc. can become a conduit through which the angels and our departed children speak to us, comfort us and help us get through this difficult time. Nevertheless, we have to start by choosing to seek these inspiring thoughts, memories and materials.

While my son had been alive, he had chosen a song that would be our song, called "Somewhere Out There." After he died I remembered his sweetness in choosing it for me, and it became an essential part of my "collection" of inspiring materials that could help pick me up when I was feeling low.

41

Pretty soon after his death, I received a sign from Christopher letting me know that he was around and okay; it was through this very song.

This was very strange for me. After all, I have a bachelor's degree in biochemistry and therefore considered myself to be very skeptical. Well, all of that began to change quickly after Christopher died. A few weeks after his death, I was at a Hallmark store when I came across a beautiful lacquered box that drew me in. As I went closer to take a look, I noticed it had a little boy sitting on a crescent moon, painting a star. Then, I realized it was not just a pretty box, but a music box. When I turned it around and saw the song it played, I just knew it was not only meant for me but that it had been handpicked by Christopher to be my Christmas gift. It played the song he had declared to be our song when he was six years old: "Somewhere Out There" sung by Linda Ronstadt. These kinds of things started to happen and opened a door to my learning to notice that magical things were taking place in my life and that my child was determined to let me know he was still around and his love is eternal.

My point in sharing this is that in becoming a collector of objects, sayings, books, poems, feathers, anything that you feel drawn toward and that makes you feel lighter, you are giving a powerful message to the unseen, to God, to your child, to the

Angels, that you are open to receiving even more inspiring and uplifting messages that nurture your relationship with your child and the spiritual world and that you are ready to move from the winter of your deepest grief to the spring of renewal and healing. It all starts with noticing the shimmering in the snow.

Christopher's Christmas Gift

Selene Negrette

.

Chapter 5 – A Patch of Blue in the Skies

"And once the storm is over, you won't remember how you made it through,
how you managed to survive. ... But one thing is certain.
When you come out of the storm, you won't be the same person who walked in.
That's what this storm's all about."

— Haruki Murakami

When as parents we are faced with the loss of our child, our whole lives are turned topsy-turvy and life as we knew it ends. As we navigate the cold, wintery landscape of our grief and notice the snow sometimes shimmers, we may be soothed and comforted in that fleeting moment, but we need more to go on. We need some lasting guidance and direction to fully assimilate who we are now because we are never again going to be the person we were before the loss of our child. We may have begun to use tools, but we feel the need to push further to greater clarity. The way I like to put it is that we need a little patch of blue in our sky, to show us there is still a wide horizon beyond waiting for our new selves to greet it.

I used to be timid, an observer in this world. I was also in awe of the medical professionals' expertise and worried about what others thought of me. I strived to do my best at everything: to be the best mother, the best wife, the best friend. I wanted very much to look good in the eyes of others. All of those ways of being fell entirely by the wayside after Christopher's diagnosis. Did something like this happen to you too? Did your sleeping tigress come to life — as it she did for me — and became extremely protective and outspoken because you wanted to make sure your child was okay? Did you begin to speak your mind and even disagree with the doctors and nurses taking care of your child because you realized that you were the expert on your child, not them? Did you stop caring about what others thought? Changes like this are completely normal; I went through them too and became someone I really could not recognize from before my son's illness. They happened out of necessity and because I needed to survive. I didn't ask for this, and in all truth, I still wish time could go backwards to erase his diagnosis so that I would still have him with me today in this moment. I wouldn't mind being less strong, less empowered, if only I had him back here with me.

Part of the reason we struggle so much to move forward after the loss of our child is that we may not *want* to move forward; what we probably want in our heart of hearts is to move backwards to the point before the start of everything leading up to our child's death, whether by illness, accident, suicide or murder. However, deep in our hearts we know that we *must* for the sake of our families, our other children — if we have them — and our own sake.

The truth is, the grief that fills our hearts after the loss of a child is so immense, it obliterates everything, including the desire to live. I think that in some way, we parents feel that if we decide to live again, we deny our child's existence or we will forget our child or others will forget our child. What I came to realize was that if I asked myself, "What would Christopher want me to do?", I knew he would want me to live again and do something positive, helpful and healing to others — out of such a sad and immense sense of loss. But the truth is, I just couldn't do so initially. I was too heartbroken, too sad and numb to want to do anything. Eventually, I slowly took small, baby steps, using many of the tools and practices already discussed so far. The timing of when a bereaved parent is ready to begin to live again is very personal and cannot be hurried. It is important to focus on muddling through life one day at a time until you reach the point of readiness to learn how to live again. Having said that, if you felt drawn to reading this book, chances are you are ready. Do you think you can do it? If not, trust me. You can do this, and you know how I know that? Because I did, and if I could, so can you!

One very important step you can take is to come to terms with the fact that your loss has profoundly changed you and the coping skills you used in the past to deal with your stresses do not work anymore. Why? Because you are not the same. Here is an example of how changed we, the bereaved parents, can be as a result of our loss:

Melissa

A single mother of three young children, Melissa worked hard to provide for all of their needs. One day, she found out she was pregnant again. Even though her pregnancy was uneventful, her baby boy was born with a congenital condition that compromised his life and made it necessary for Melissa to quit her job to care for him. Financially, that step was very scary for her. It made life much more stressful as she had to go on welfare and rely on her child's social security income to survive and provide for all of her children. Melissa had taken pride in her ability to provide before her baby was born. It was very difficult for her to ask for help from her family, friends or neighbors. After he was born with such complex health issues, she lived in constant fear of him dying and her other children complained because she did not spend as much time with them. When their baby brother was in the hospital, they had to stay with relatives. They missed the mother they had had before. Melissa felt constantly torn between caring for her very ill baby and making sure that her other children's needs were attended to. Needless to say, her other children suffered. When she finally reached out for help and began to use some of the tools in here, she realized her predominant feeling was one of anger because she felt that it was not fair for her baby to be so sick and for her to have to struggle so much in life. She began to write in a journal, and it was cathartic and helpful to her. When her baby died suddenly, she found herself unable to go on initially, but her fear of losing her other children to foster care helped her do what she needed to do for their sake. Melissa began to dwell on the gift that it was to have had her baby for four years, especially considering the doctors had told her he would not live longer than a few months. As she concentrated on blessing the time she had her child, she began to feel less angry and became more functional. With the support of her family, she was able to go back to work a few months after her child's death and found bereavement groups for her children as well as for herself. She became aware of the fact that her experience of loss had profoundly changed her and the trusting and self-sufficient woman she had been before no longer existed. Now, she was not so trusting, especially in the health care system; she also felt much more vulnerable and had had to learn to ask for help; otherwise, she would not have been able to live again.

Do you see how realizing that she was not the same person she was before her loss helped Melissa see that she needed different ways of coping, such as asking for help from others? And how that realization together with her commitment to taking action started her on the path to moving forward?

Exercise: Old You vs. New You

One very important step you can take is to come to terms with the fact that your loss has profoundly changed you. Your old coping skills do not work anymore. Why? Because you are not the same. How much have you changed? You are about to find out...

The Old You

Have you taken time to look back at your old life? The things that made you happy then, the way you related to your friends, family, husband and children? How about the activities you enjoyed most or the problems that kept you up at night? Take a pen to paper and begin to reflect on the old you. I created a worksheet you can follow if you feel like it can help you at this time. Answer each question as honestly and completely as possible. Remember, this is for you!

50

Your Life Before

1. Did you consider yourself to be a happy person before?
2. Were you holding a job or staying at home?
3. Were you satisfied with your life?
4. Did you have a loving and close relationship with your husband?
5. Did you derive great joy from parenting, even though you found it difficult at times?
6. Did you have several close and supportive friends?
7. Did you have a good relationship with your family? Your parents? Your siblings?
8. Did you have a church family which supported and nourished you spiritually?
9. What were your major concerns before?
10. In what direction did you envision your life moving before?

Here is another example of how vastly the loss of a child can change our lives:

Julia

Julia had just lost her only child, a daughter, to cancer. Devastated and paralyzed, she felt she had lost everything. Her life had revolved around caring for her daughter, her activities and her wishes; now, all that was gone. She loved being a mother and giving to her daughter. Understandably, she felt robbed and was angry at the world for leaving her with nothing to give her life meaning. Slowly, Julia began to realize that in order to wake up from her zombie state, she had to look at life differently because she was different. At first, she recognized she was filled with a sense of outrage and anger at the world for robbing her of who she loved most; she tried to feel differently but came to the conclusion she had to allow herself to feel what she felt without judging. As she did more and more of this allowing, over time she was writing down her feelings and decided to take out all the photos that held memories of her life with her daughter. She found her mood lifting as she looked at all the love, joy, vitality and beauty in her daughter's eyes. In dwelling on those memories, she felt her anger slowly dissipate. She did not have a daughter to take care of any longer, but she would always be her mother and she could find a way to keep their connection alive in order to find a new way to live. After she had that realization, she took active steps to pick up the pieces of her life. Her awareness of spirituality had developed since her daughter's illness. Before, Julia had needed concreteness and solidity. Afterwards, she began to see what she needed most was to pay attention to the signs her daughter was leaving her to let her know that she was okay and that she loved her. In becoming aware of this, Julia started to hone in on her own spiritual gifts to feel her daughter's presence around her. She realized that even though her child had died, she could continue to parent her; she could continue the relationship, and this would be healing to her. Julia now feels that, with her daughter's help, she can craft a path in life that will allow her to help others. Sometimes, she shakes her head as she looks back at her old self, someone who would never have been able to believe in angels or spiritual connections to her child who passed. Julia is also able to feel grateful for her new self's openness to this expansive view of seeing life.

The New You

No other experience has the potential to totally change you more than the loss of a child. Why is that? Because it defies everything we know and believe in. Children are not supposed to die. And when they do, nobody has answers for you or they have unhelpful answers. When as a parent you have faced this and find yourself in the midst of unspeakable grief, what do you do? What *can* you do?

One thing you can do is take quiet time to think about how different you are from who you were before your loss. Think about all the different areas of your life that have changed, about your view on life, relationships, parenting, work, etc. Write them all down and reflect on the fact that you have been a warrior who went to battle, and even though you came back defeated, you also came back much stronger and with many lessons that can help you deal with whatever life throws at you. Here is the worksheet I have created to help you come to terms with the changes you have gone through and connect with the new version of yourself you now are.

Your Life After

1. What would you say your main emotional state is like?

2. Are you able to hold a job or are you staying at home? Would you like to be able to work but are feeling incapacitated at this time?

3. Would you say you are satisfied with your current life?

4. In what ways has the death of your child affected your relationship with your spouse? Are you closer or farther apart from one another?

5. How do you feel about parenting your children if you have any? Is it a constant struggle? Is it a distraction that helps you at times?

6. Have your friends remained by your side or have you lost some and gained new ones during the journey?

7. In what ways has your relationship with your family been affected? Are you feeling closer or less close to your parents or your siblings?

8. How has this experience affected your spirituality or religious beliefs?

9. What are your main concerns at this time?

10. In which direction do you see your life moving after the loss?

Now, put the two lists side by side to compare the Old You versus the New You. This should help you see in a more concrete way just how changed you are. You can then use the information to find ways to cope. That realization is the patch of blue in the skies of your life; it is a small sign of hope that you are beginning to find your way.

Parents tell me all the time that not only do they not recognize themselves but their family and friends also comment on how much more outspoken, less patient with petty concerns and struggles, less worried about what other people think, or how much their priorities have changed. They also tell me that even though they feel exhausted, sad and angry, they also feel more resilient and know that if they survived the loss of their child, they can survive anything.

Spirituality and Bereaved Parents

The New You of many bereaved parents, myself included, may usher changes in spirituality. A common thread is the experience of non-ordinary phenomena: signs and messages the child leaves for their parents to reassure them and convey they are around and still love them. More often than not, the parents had not been open to believing or being aware of these type of experiences. What does this mean? It means a ray of hope enters their consciousness to inform them it is possible to keep the connection they had with their child alive, even after their death.

I remember vividly my first experiences with my own child. About three weeks after his death, I had a dream that felt more like a visit: He was younger than when he died and his hair had grown back a little —it was at the stage I loved it the most, soft just like a duckling's down— and he was wearing a white t-shirt. He led me into a white room with a large, white bed and motioned for me to sit by him. He held a little, brown book he was going to read to me when I woke up. It felt wonderful to experience my son again, even if in a dream.

I relate to all the bereaved parents who share some of these types of experiences, messages, signs, songs, etc. with their family members and friends, only to receive looks of disbelief. I want you to know that your experiences are *real*, that you are not imagining them or creating them to feel better or to keep the connection to your child alive. Trust your instincts that tell you without a shadow of a doubt that it is your child and they are lovingly letting you know that love is eternal and never dies.

It has now been twenty-one years since Christopher died and I still receive signs from him, such as a monarch butterfly that decides to stick around for a long time, happily dancing in front of me and showing up exactly when I'm feeling down, worried or in need of guidance; a feather that suddenly lands on the ground right in front of me. These are signs from my son that help me know he is still with me after all this time, and I cannot fully put into words how instrumental my awareness of this ongoing connection has been in my own journey of healing, growth and transformation.

I have no doubt that it will play a significant role in your own journey as well. Here is what one of my clients experienced:

Maria

Maria is an exceptional woman and mother. She has two daughters. One of them died a few months ago, and the other is adjusting to life without her sister with the support and guidance of her mother. Maria was the number one fan of her daughter who died. She fought tooth and nail for her life and kept strong for her sake, even though Maria was crumbling to pieces inside. When she died, Maria fell apart. Most days she felt she could not get out of bed or tend to the needs of her other child. She knew she had to for her living daughter's sake. So she made herself do it — do something to try to get herself out of her grief. She started visiting her daughter's grave and having long conversations with her. She asked her for a sign that she was okay. One day at the gravesite, Maria felt someone staring at her, and when she turned around, she saw a large bunny — a notoriously skittish animal — sitting quite close and staring at her. The bunny had come out of nowhere and was intent on capturing her attention. It allowed her to pet him and looked so lovingly at her that she had the sudden realization that this was her daughter's sign. She had loved rabbits and her pet rabbit Cuddles was still at home. Maria realized her daughter's love for her was so powerful that it could make something like that happen for her sake. That was only the beginning of many more messages and signs that kept coming and bringing slowly but surely more healing to this wonderful mother's heart.

Chapter 6 – Footprints in the Snow

"Acknowledge your inner child. Even though we have found the light in ourselves today, we sometimes forget to heal old wounds of our past. Your inner child still needs to be loved in order to heal the complete self."

— Karen A. Baquiran

When we bereaved parents grieve, we are not only grieving for the loss of our child, we are also grieving — whether we realize it or not — for all the accumulated hurts and losses we have experienced throughout our lives up to that point in time. Our grief offers us an opportunity to heal those other wounds. The way I look at it is that we are unable to move because our hearts are so burdened. That is why I call this step, "Footprints in the Snow," because as we unburden our hearts from our childhood wounds and hurts, we become light enough to move toward healing, and with this healing, we make space in our hearts for more love toward ourselves first which will, in turn, benefit all those whom we love.

If you have other children and are a bereaved parent, one of your biggest concerns is raising and helping them grieve. However, before you can help your other children, there is another child who needs your attention first; that is the child within you. It is very important to ask yourself, "What are the unmet needs and/or wounds I am still carrying from my childhood?" so that you can attend to them now. Nobody else can do this for you; this is something you need to do for yourself and by yourself. This is how you come to give yourself the love you need. Once you do this, a lot of your struggles will begin to fall by the wayside; by this I mean, that you will begin to care for and honor yourself first before anybody else and you will know deep inside that doing that is not a selfish thing to do but instead, it is the most loving thing you can do, for yourself *and* for others. The truth of the matter is that unless we come from a place of fullness in our self-love, we can't truly love others.

You are probably thinking: how on earth am I going to do this when I am in such a depleted state? And my answer is, you need to do this precisely *because* you are in such a depleted state. Connecting to your inner child's needs has the potential of being another spark to fuel your healing process, so it is a truly worthy endeavor.

I will share with you now the way I came to this realization. I was feeling deeply sad practically every day after Christopher died, and my most prevalent thoughts were of how sorry I felt for myself. I did not have anybody to help me as I navigated the murky waters of grief and did not have the energy to ask for help. So I kept pushing myself and pushing myself until the day I came face to face with my inner child's need to be loved and receive approval from my father. It happened during a phone conversation with him when I realized I had been carrying around this wish for approval from him since I was a little girl. I came to terms with the fact that, as a grown woman, I needed to let go of that need. In fact, not healing that childhood wound was actually holding me back from healing in my grief process over my son; it was also limiting the quality of love I was giving to my children, to my husband, etc. because I was not coming from a place of fullness inside of me, but from a place of want and need that had been there since childhood. That day I made a promise to myself to accept the fact that my father did not consciously withhold his love or approval, he simply was not able to give it. He did the best he could even though it was not enough for me. I was able to release that need and let it go as I forgave him; the relief I felt was immense. When you heal a childhood wound, the benefits reverberate throughout every area of your life. My ability to give love to my children, my family, friends and especially myself skyrocketed afterward. And that was just the beginning of me having a loving relationship with myself. It is very rare now when I find myself feeling sorry for myself because I know I have the power to take control over my life, to look within to heal what needs to be healed. I do not mean to say it is wrong to feel sorry for yourself. It is normal to do so after something as tragic and sad as the loss of one's child; what I mean is, if you find yourself doing this for days and months on end, then it is time to look within so you can find out what wounds are lurking from your childhood so you can make room for positive changes. Are you ready to do this in your own life? I promise you will not regret it!

Why Is Self-Nurturing So Important?

As mothers, loving our children usually comes naturally. Giving of ourselves to them is something we want to do and makes us feel better as human beings as well. As bereaved mothers, we have given of ourselves to care for our child and other children until we could no longer do so. The point when we hit that wall was when our child died. So what can we do? Well, this is when I think all of the practices I have discussed can come in handy because they allow you to focus on YOU for once. In doing that, they nudge you to offer compassion, understanding and love to yourself. And when you begin to do that, whether by carving out a time during the day which is yours and yours alone, or scheduling a weekly girls lunch date, or taking steps to schedule a massage or a mani-pedi on a regular basis, you begin to move from feeling dry and unable to care for others, to feeling fuller and lighter and able to give of yourself to those who need you and count on you for their care and well-being. The big difference now is, you will be doing so from a place of *fullness*, not of depletion.

Here are some steps you can take to come face to face with your unmet needs:

Old Childhood Photos

Look through your closets and drawers until you find several of your photos as a child. Put them in front of you as you go back in time in your mind's eye to remember what it was like to be you at the age you were in each photo. What were you doing in the photo? What things did you look forward to the most? How did you feel about your mother, your father, your siblings? Did you have close friends? Do any of the photos bring out sad memories or feelings of hurt within you? Take notes of everything that comes to your mind. After you have done this, it is time to write a letter or record a conversation with your inner child. Offer him or her your sympathy, understanding and give him or her love.

Writing Letters

Write a letter to your inner child. Offer compassion, love and full understanding. Explain the reasons why his or her needs were not fully met and encourage that inner child to try to forgive the person or people who hurt him or her so that you, the adult, can take a step forward, feeling lighter and more full of love in your heart. After you do this, place the letter in a glass jar or a metal can and burn it to symbolize that you are letting go. You may have to do this several times, as different hurts at different ages and with different people come to your mind. There is no rush. Take your time because this process takes a lot out of you emotionally. Keep in mind that you buried these hurts as a child because you could not deal with them, and now, when you are in the depths of your grief, you are excavating them out to air so you can heal. Also, you may begin this process and abandon it for several months. That's okay. The important thing here is, you are slowly but surely taking action to heal and feel better, lighter and more self-loving.

Making a List

You take care of past hurts by writing them down and letting them go. But what do you do with the unmet needs you have identified? List them and take care of them yourself one at a time. For example, if as a child you did not get enough attention because your parents favored your oldest sister; you can offer that attention to yourself. Hold conversations with yourself in front of the mirror and tell yourself just how worthy of people's attention you are; tell yourself you are a lovely person who is interesting and charming, a magnet to others who freely give you their attention. This may seem silly, but it is actually a very powerful practice and I invite you to give it a try.

Here's an example that illustrates why it is important to get in touch with our unmet needs/wounds in order to heal:

Carina

Carina is a loving mother of three children. She had given of herself time and time again to her children, her husband and her family. However, after her oldest child died, a little girl, she found herself in a vicious cycle of sadness, resentment and hurt. She began to write to her inner child and realized that as a child she had not received the love she had needed. As a result, she had developed a pattern of giving of herself, her time and energy to other people to the point of absolute exhaustion. Her sense of self-worth was rooted in her constant role as a giver, and without it, she did not feel she *could* be loved, much less love herself. She had given all she had to her daughter who died and was continuing to do so with her other children, but she did not have anything left to give to her husband or her family. In having conversations with herself, she was able to offer love, understanding and compassion to her inner child to heal the wounds of not having been loved unconditionally. This helped her give herself permission to inform her husband, family and friends when she needed to replenish and be by herself or when she wanted to do things for herself and by herself. She told me she had never given herself permission to be good to herself and that it was very healing for her to do so. Why? Because it allowed her to be more loving toward her family and not feel depleted all the time when doing for others. Taking steps to heal and nurture one's inner child is something I equate to the beginning of leaving "Footprints in the Snow" as you journey to your own healing.

Chapter 7 – The Bridge

"There's this place in me where your fingerprints still rest,
your kisses still linger and your whispers softly echo;
it's the place where a part of you will forever be a part of me."

— Unknown

When a child dies, a family loses its axis and has to find it again while going through the painful process of grieving. The bereaved parents become incapacitated, and if there are siblings, they are left, oftentimes, feeling lost and in need of direction. However, the love bereaved parents have for their children can be the bridge to taking the steps they need to take to continue in their journey of healing. That is why I call this step, "The Bridge." (If you are a bereaved parent who has lost her or his only child, I address this later in the chapter.)

As bereaved parents, we may feel dead inside, but we will do anything in the world to make sure our grieving children are okay, and we will scrape the earth if necessary to help them. It is the love we have for our children that helps us parents bridge the space from our inner winter state to the emerging possibility that we may someday feel the sun of spring again.

How the adults around our children, including ourselves as parents, react to the death determine how our other children, in turn, react and grieve. It is important to allow open acknowledgement of the grief, to convey it is normal to feel sad on the inside and the outside and to cry often. What children need most is the reassurance that someone is still in charge and that it is safe to ask questions and ask for emotional support. What children do *not* need is to feel that they need to take care of their parents. Remember, they are still kids and need to continue to be allowed to be kids. This is not the time to ask them to grow up.

What does this mean for us parents? It means it is very important to make sure we have a good support system made up of people we can go to when we need to fall apart, or need help with household chores, or anything that will help us keep our sanity. In leaning on this support system, we can be as present as we can for our children.

I know that after Christopher died, my main concern was how to help his brother and sister. They were seven and four years old, respectively, and I wanted to make sure they did receive all the support they needed. One of the things I did early on was make each of them a small photo album filled with pictures of them with their brother Christopher to keep on their nightstand and have at the ready to look at when they missed their brother. I also had them choose a stuffed animal and/or toy they wanted from Christopher's stash that they could sleep with, play with and keep for always. Now that my children are grown, they tell me how much both of those symbolic mementos of their brother meant to them.

Expect the behavior of your children to change with grief, as the loss has traumatized them. During the first few months and possibly the first year, I would listen to my kids play, and it always involved somebody dying, either a dinosaur or a doll; this is the way children process death and incorporate it into their lives. Also, their drawings at school showed what was foremost on their minds. I remember finding a drawing my seven-year-old made in school of his brother in a casket. Another of his drawings was a house and a huge, dark tornado coming directly toward it. It made me feel sad, but at the same time, I knew it was good for him to have that creative outlet for his thoughts and feelings. That was how it felt to him, and that needed to be honored, not stifled.

Children cope differently, depending on their age, personality, type of loss, family circumstances and development, so we as parents need to be very attuned to each child's unique ways of grieving. With my son and daughter, for example, it was important for me to identify what each of them needed so I could determine the best way to help them through their grief. My son kept his feelings to himself and mostly stayed quiet while missing his brother very deeply; my daughter, on the other hand, was very open and angry about her feelings. She demanded that if God took her brother to heaven, why could we not get a tall ladder, go up there and bring him back? She was furious, and of course, being four years old, she did not fully grasp that death was a permanent thing. She talked about him all the time and had conversations with him while I was driving in the car. My son expressed his feelings through his drawings at school and enacting deaths at playtime. Because he was not talkative with me about his grief — more than likely protecting me — I took him to see a grief counselor to make sure he had someone he felt comfortable talking about Christopher with. After three months, the counselor told me he was coping very healthily with his grief. From time to time, my son would ask me to hold him on my lap and rock him in the rocking chair. I would do that for him as he was obviously in need of extra nurturing. Moreover, both of my children asked to sleep in my room for several years after their brother died. I allowed it because I knew they needed the closeness and comfort. Slowly, they began to want to go to their room and sleep in their own beds; eventually, they stopped coming to my room when they were ready. This was all part of a healthy healing process, and it was important that I offer them the nurturing, understanding and support I myself needed. After all, we had gone on a journey of loss together!

Their Lives Before

While it's true that we ourselves feel we are no longer the same person after our child's death, it is also true that the experience has fundamentally changed our other children. If we try to put ourselves in their shoes, we will find they must have felt very confused by all the changes that happened in their lives because of the loss of their sibling. The anguish they witness in their parents affects them greatly because our children love us so much that if we suffer, they suffer. It is very important to talk with them and explain *why* we are sad. In having these conversations, we give them permission to also be sad, and we treat them with the respect they deserve. Children are so much more resilient than we think. They can take any kind of news we give them, as long as we take the time to explain to them what has happened, even if we don't have any answers, and we assure them they are not alone and they can come to us with any questions, feelings or concerns.

In my work, I have come to realize that bereaved children have had to spend a lot of time eavesdropping to gather the information they needed to make sense of what was happening in their little world — where there may have been lightheartedness and ease before, they see the strained faces of their parents, hushed conversations or crying. As a result, they become master eavesdroppers. Wouldn't it be nice if we made it easier for them by openly providing them with the information they needed? In that way, we would spare them from having to experience any anxiety due to possibly misconstruing what they have overheard. We would also help them stop protecting the adults in their lives as they come to realize they can come to us with their fears and worries.

I know that in my own experience, my children had gone to war with me as we fought for Christopher's life, but because I was so wrapped up in making sure he had all his medications and treatments so he would survive, I failed to notice what was going on with my other children. I can't torture myself about that because I was truly doing the best I could at the time, and as a bereaved parent yourself, I ask that you don't blame yourself for not always having been perfect. When you find yourself doing that, blaming yourself or being self-deprecating, please close your eyes and remind yourself of your deep love for your children. Recognize that you did the best that you could at the time. Have you ever tried hugging yourself? It's a very powerful practice. So, go ahead and hug yourself and offer yourself some love every time you are being hard on yourself.

What ended up happening to me was that after Christopher died, I realized my children had been like little baby birds sitting in a nest. I had three birds: Christopher, Jonathan and Elise. Christopher, who was gravely ill, had never had any difficulty voicing his needs so his needs were attended to, especially as he needed me so much more due to his illness; Elise, my youngest, also had no trouble speaking up for herself; however, Jonathan, my middle child, was the sweet little bird sitting on the nest looking at me with pleading eyes, hoping that I would notice he needed something from me, but because he wasn't making any noise, I didn't notice and so his needs did not get met as they should have. Of course, once I realized this, I began to get in touch with his *particular* way of communicating — always non-verbal — his needs to me and was able to provide him with the reassurance and attention he needed.

I don't think I am alone in having had to put my other children on the back-burner to attend to my sick child. What I want you to realize is that the siblings' lives are as destroyed as yours from their sibling's death, and what you need, they also need. So the best way to help them is to ask yourself, what do I need? And then give that to yourself first and to them second. In my case, I needed so much nurturing after Christopher's death; I needed for someone to listen to me as I talked about my son who had died and to acknowledge he had existed. So, instead of avoiding the subject like it was too painful, I began to talk about Christopher with my children all the time. They liked to talk about him; he continued to be present in their lives, in their games, in their minds and hearts as he also was in mine. In a sense, I allowed my children to be the bridge for me, and it was a beautiful part of our joined healing process.

Memory Affirming Activities

As parents, we know our children best and therefore, we can select what sort of activities our children will respond to the best. I will share with you some I did with my own children as well as some of the ones I have encouraged other parents to try with their kids.

1. If your child was able to say goodbye to their brother or sister: Just the memory of having been able to say "I love you" one last time will be very healing to the child. However, you can also ask if they would like to have one of the toys, stuffed animals or a t-shirt from the child who died to hold onto. You can also arrange for someone to make a stuffed animal from an item of clothing belonging to the child who died as a special memento.

2. If your child was not able to say goodbye: Coming up with a ritual to symbolically say goodbye can be both helpful and healing. You can encourage your child/children to write a letter or make a drawing to say goodbye. Just writing the letter is a wonderful outlet for the emotions, but to take it a step further, you can tell your child that the Native Americans believed that if your burn a message, the smoke would carry it to their loved ones who had passed on. If they like the idea, you can proceed together to burn it in the fireplace or in a tin can or a glass jar. This is very powerful and can bring up bottled up emotions within your child, so be prepared with tissues, a blanket and lots of hugs. You can also join your children in writing a letter yourself as well and burn them all at the same time.

3. You don't have to wait for the anniversary of your child's death or their birthday to take your children to the gravesite, you can do so at any time. One beautiful practice I used with my own family is very simple but powerfully symbolic and healing. Buy regular balloons from a store (have the children pick out the color) and ask each sibling to write a note to the child who died on a piece of paper, which you can then attach to each balloon. Release the balloons and tell your children the message is going to their deceased brother/sister. Symbolic rituals such as this are very therapeutic, and

children with their active imaginations easily grasp their meaning and benefit from them.

4. You can also have quiet time with them by bringing a photo album and encourage your children to talk about their brother/sister. Go down memory lane together as you recollect all sorts of memories: some sad, some funny, some touching, others happy. Make sure you hug your children and reassure them they were and still are *great* siblings to their brother/sister.

When to Worry

Children tend to show the world how they are feeling by how they behave. Tantrums in the home, misbehaving in school, stealing or getting in fights or in trouble at school are all signs of your child having great difficulty making sense of the loss. If this happens, the most important thing to keep in mind is that your child is crying for attention, *your* attention, due to a need to be nurtured. So, giving of your time to talk with them, giving them permission to show their feelings to you and/or to talk about their sibling who passed, reassuring them it will not make you sadder to talk about their brother/sister are all extremely important. In addition, it is essential to find out if your child is feeling guilty for having felt, at some point or other, that they wished their brother or sister had died. Children need to be told that they did *not* make their sibling die because of what they were thinking at one particular moment, and they also need to hear it is common for siblings to wish things like that from time to time — it does not make them a bad person. If you feel you are not able to provide all the nurturing/attention your child needs, make sure to enlist relatives and friends to help you. Being completely honest with yourself as to what you are able to provide is essential. Do not feel bad about asking others to help out. The most loving thing you can do is to make sure your children always have someone they can rely on for support, even if it is not 100% of the time, as this is key to helping your child face the future in spite of their loss. If none of these things help, make sure you take your child to a grief counselor because if grief is left unattended, it will have repercussions in your child's adult life and relationships. Support groups where children can meet other children who have lost a sibling can be very helpful in normalizing their grief, because more likely than not, your children do not have any friends or classmates in school who have had the same kind of loss.

Another key thing to keep in mind is that even though the birth order (oldest, middle, youngest) of your children is now different because of the death, the surviving children cannot be expected to take on a different order. For example, if the child who died was the oldest, we cannot expect the middle child to assume the role of the child who died. The siblings will eventually find their own sense of identity, but as parents we cannot pressure them. Another thing we cannot do is to idealize the child who died. Something quite important is to make sure that when we have conversations with our children about the child who died, we present a balanced picture of the good things and the not so good things about our child so that we do not push our other children into a complex of trying to be perfect to compete with the idealized image of their sibling.

When *Not* to Worry

If your child talks about their sibling in spurts and then goes on with playing, this is normal and the way most children grieve. The fact that they are talking and/or expressing their feelings — acknowledging they are sad or missing their sibling — is a healthy sign of the normal grieving.

If your child is clingier, needier or more fearful than usual, this is also normal, but it signals that as parents we may need to make allowances and not expect the normal routines or guidelines of the household to be followed at this time. For example, if allowing our child in your bed was a "no-no" before, then perhaps now, it would benefit your child to be allowed to snuggle with you because they need additional nurturing and care. In time, possibly weeks or months, your child will *want* to return to their bed. If your child is afraid, it is helpful to explore the reasons why. Is your child afraid they may also die? Are they afraid that you may die? Having a conversation about any of your child's fears or concerns allows you to provide much-needed reassurance and signals to them that you are here to protect them and that you are taking great care of yourself so your child does not need to worry on your account. You can also incorporate a prayer to God or to the child who died that you can say together, asking for protection for your child/children and your family. In doing this, you are taking action by introducing a ritual that can provide reassurance to your child, rather than just providing words. Children need concrete ways to make sense of their world, and it's up to you to provide these for them.

Nurturing the Bond with the Child Who Died

As our children grapple with making sense of a life that does not include their brother or sister, we the parents can be instrumental in helping them maintain and nurture the bond they have with their deceased sibling. How can we do so, you may be asking yourself? I will share the way in which one of the parents I know was able to do this successfully, and it proved to be very healing for her child and for her as well.

Marguerite

She was a young mother of two girls. The youngest died six months ago, and she was deep in grief and felt she could not go on because of how much she missed her daughter. However, she felt just as strongly, and I know that this resonates with you, about helping her surviving little girl at this time. The way Marguerite kept the sisterly bond alive was to have conversations at bedtime with the daughter who died. At first, her living daughter did not know what to make of listening to her mother have conversations with her deceased sister; she would say funny things, ask her for strength to go on, tell her how much she loved and missed her, etc. At first, the girl just listened to her mother, but soon she began to lead the conversations, asking her sister for help and strength and to help their mother. She also began to share what was happening in her life. When Marguerite shared this with me, she became tearful, but these were good tears because she knew that her maternal love had led her to find a way to help her daughter deal with such a terrible loss, and she also knew that this practice will help her forever by nurturing the bond between her daughters.

The Loss of an Only Child

We can all agree that the loss of a child is the worst loss. Now, the loss of an only child compounds the grief because oftentimes parents feel they do not have anything to live for, now that their sole child is gone. At least, if you have other children, you can focus on helping them, and in doing so, you end up helping yourself. I know that is just how I felt. I felt I did not want to live after Christopher's death, but the fact I had two other children who needed me was the motivating factor that kept me going forward even though I did not want to. So, how can a parent who has lost an only child survive? I found an article written by a mother whose only child, a son, committed suicide. Maria Bradshaw wrote it for the website madinamerica.com; it is titled, "How to Parent a Dead Child." In it, Ms. Bradshaw talks about how she has incorporated her son in her life by continuing to parent him. She is doing this by continuing to bake a cake on his birthday, by displaying a laminated photo of her son in her car and holding conversations with him or singing to him, and she is also taking steps to make a difference in the world for his sake. She started a charity to provide support to families bereaved by suicide, and she feels an immense sense of fulfillment by saying his name every time she talks in front of others or tells his story. She also talks to him and asks for his help when she is trying to help other parents who have lost a child to suicide.

Ms. Bradshaw is a shining example of the fact that the love we share with our children is eternal and survives death. If you have lost your only child, know that your love for your child can be its own kind of bridge to help you over the abyss of grief. Staying in touch with the fact that your child is still present in your life, though invisibly, will go a long way to helping you heal. Developing practices that keep you feeling close to him or her in daily life, like Ms. Bradshaw does, will ultimately best serve to help you cross over into a new phase of being, where hope and life begin to resurface in your world.

Chapter 8 – Grass Underfoot

"I bequeath myself to the dirt to grow from the grass I love, if you want me again
look for me under your boot soles. ... Missing me one place search another,
I stop somewhere waiting for you."

— *Walt Whitman*

The loss of a child ushers a different phase in the lives of all involved. It shakes us to the core of our existence. As we allow the love we have for our children to be the bridge that lead us to the return of spring to our lives, we also begin to have "aha" moments; things become clearer. How so? Well, for one, our relationships may have experienced tremendous changes. We have lost friendships in the process, your relationship with certain family members may have become strained, and your marital or romantic relationship may have grown distant or even closer. I call this step "Grass Underfoot," because with clarity, we can take steps toward making decisions conducive to our peace of mind and heart. That could mean we need to make more time for our spouse or romantic partner, or it could mean that divorce is the only way we *can* continue to live. Either way, if you are following this process, at this point you are coming out of the wintery landscape and can feel grass under your feet. And the grass is green! The color of hope! Why? Because you are beginning to be more clear about who you are, about how you feel and about what you truly need in your life.

When we grieve, we also have so much fear. Having to consider ending a relationship is exhausting and brings to the fore so many fears, such as, "How am I going to make it financially, or emotionally?"; "How will these further changes affect the children?"; "How can I even begin to take steps to do this when I am feeling so depleted?"

As parents, we may take the path of least resistance and stay out of each other's way as we grieve and see how it goes. It does not matter what you do as long as you are not harming yourself in the process.

The statistics vary widely on the percentage of bereaved parents who divorce after the death of their child; some say it is as high as 90%, others say it is as low as 16%. Obviously, this is a complicated issue because there are so many variables. For example, what was the state of the marriage *prior* to the loss? What was the nature of the loss? Is there blame being attached to one of the parents? What is their support system? Regardless of these details, it has to be acknowledged on a whole that the loss of a child places a huge strain on any relationship — marital, romantic, friendship, familial, etc. In regard to a marital/romantic relationship, one factor in this strain comes from the fact that, most commonly, men and women grieve in very different ways, which can seem incomprehensible and frustrating to one another and which can create a shut-down barrier for any communication that could help the marriage/relationship survive. Here, I am going to outline some of the general types of grief to shed some light into the complex and different ways in which people grieve:

Intuitive Grief

Parents who are intuitive grievers tend to feel their grief very intensely. They may cry very often and do so in a very open and free way because that is what they need to do to process their feelings. Many women are intuitive grievers, but some men grieve in this way as well.

Instrumental Grief

Some parents cope by focusing less on their feelings and instead channel their grief into more physical solutions. For example, these parents might think of what they can do or how they can problem-solve. They are usually not very open to discussing their feelings because that is not very helpful to them. Many fathers cope by doing, by taking care of chores or immersing themselves in their jobs more and pushing their feelings aside; this is very helpful to them. It doesn't mean they are not grieving; what it does mean is they are doing it in a way most helpful to them. Some women cope in this way as well.

Blended Grief

Some parents cope by showing characteristics of both types of grievers. This makes sense because each individual is very unique and their ways of coping are even more so.

How Most Women Grieve

Woman tend to grieve more openly, to abandon themselves to their feelings, and in expressing them, they feel a great relief. Crying openly and at many times throughout the day is very cathartic and a necessity for many women who have lost a child. This behavior is supported by society. Also, if the woman has been the main caregiver and involved more in the day-to-day activities of their child, such as grocery shopping, doing homework, carpooling, driving to extra-curricular activities, etc., she will feel the void her child left in her life more strongly, and this will bring more tears to her eyes on a daily basis.

How Most Men Grieve

Men tend to keep their grief to themselves because, unfortunately, most of society supports the notion that men are not supposed to cry. Also, men may feel they need to stay strong for their family and may not want to be perceived as weak. Men tend to cry when alone and often cope by keeping busy with work and other practical considerations. This is the polar opposite from what women need, and it may appear to their partner as if the man is not grieving at all; however, this is just a different way of grieving.

How Can You Help Your Husband/Partner

The most important thing you can do is understand that whatever way your husband, partner or boyfriend grieves, it is okay because that is what they need to continue to survive while grieving. To be able to suspend judgement or criticism of the other is one of the best things you can offer. Also, to make a pact that you will do everything you can to *not* expect the other to take care of each other's emotional needs at this time is very important. You are *both* depleted and the best you can do is to take care of yourselves as best you can. Having understood this, you will offer each other understanding and kindness at this time without the unnecessary burden of placing your needs onto their plate as well.

One helpful thing to offer one another is the space you need and the ability to seek a friend or relative who can support you at this time in the way that you need. Sometimes, your spouse needs to talk with someone, and that person may not necessarily be you, but rather, someone outside the situation, who can give them a more impartial view on things. Respecting and allowing that space without getting your feelings hurt allows you a chance to do the same and can ultimately help you both to have more positive conversations and interactions afterwards when you reconvene. Another thing you can do is to promise each other to keep talking about what helps and what does not help, openly and constructively, so you can offer kindness to one another and remain supportive of one another in your grief.

One of the things that can be difficult for bereaved parents is the fact that grief in males seems to decline more rapidly than in females. The grief in mothers tends to peak at around two years after the death of their child, whereas at that time, the grief in fathers' is declining. Couples or bereaved parents, they need to know and understand that this is a natural phenomenon so they can offer each other the support they need without feeling as if the other does not care or needs to move on. Acknowledging and respecting you each have your own healing process to go through with its own perfect pace is so very important.

The Importance of Respect

What is the definition of respect? It is a feeling of deep admiration for someone or something elicited by their abilities, qualities or achievements. As parents who have gone through the horrifying and heart-breaking experience of losing a child, it is of the utmost importance to be able to recognize that you both are survivors and that you both are trying in the best way you are able to, to continue living and contributing to the world even though life as you once knew it is gone. When you are able to offer each other that kind of admiration, of respect for the fact you are still here, the feeling and the experience of yourselves in the relationship has the potential of being transformed to one of kindness and understanding of each other's needs.

Healing Rituals

A good way to communicate with each other as bereaved parents is to establish a ritual. For example, you could decide to light a candle in the bedroom whenever one of you is having an especially hard day in their grief and needs some space or more understanding. This is helpful particularly when one of the parents needs to talk about feelings while the other one prefers not to. In this way you can give a wide berth to the one who is having more difficulty, and you don't need to talk about it, but you can offer them a comforting hug or hold hands. Touch can communicate a lot of caring without the need for words.

Parenting Grieving Children Through Divorce

Speaking from my own personal experience, I know that sometimes divorce is the only way to survive. In my case, my marriage was not doing well even before Christopher was diagnosed and all of the underlying frictions were exacerbated by the stresses and fears of the ongoing years of battling the cancer. I had made the conscious decision to stay with my husband for my son's sake because I did not want Christopher to have to deal with being separated from his father while undergoing his grueling treatments — and of course, I also worried about my other two children — however, in the end, I found that I could no longer hold on. We divorced five months after his death at a point in which I can say that there truly was no way in which the marriage could have been saved. I will say that even though the marriage was shaky before the diagnosis, the fact that such a terrible thing happened offered us an opportunity to become closer through the facing of adversity, but unfortunately, that was not what happened; instead, the fissure in our marriage became a large chasm that could not be breached.

By divorcing while grieving the loss of my child, my main concern had to do with my other children. Losing their brother was enough of a blow to them, but for me to take that step and add to their grief and stress by diminishing the time they were going to spend with their father was unimaginable. In the end, I had to do quite a bit of soul-searching to reach the conclusion that any step I could take toward my *own* happiness would only be a positive thing for them as well, because I would be showing them with my own actions that doing what you need to do to be happy is not selfish; it is self-love. Doing so allowed me to be the best mother I could to them and opened my heart to offering them even more love than I ever could have, had I decided to stay in such a deeply unhappy marriage. After the divorce, my task was not to feel bad about it, but rather to find a way to reassure them that both their father and I would continue to love them for the rest of their lives, even if we had to live in separate houses; that we were committed to their well-being and would always do what was necessary to help them grow and support them.

My children are grown now, and they both tell me that talking with them as openly as I did and explaining to them why the divorce happened and what it would mean for them while providing them with reassurance of my commitment and unconditional love was very healing to them and went a long way to diminishing their anxiety during such a sad and transitional time in their lives.

Chapter 9 – Wildflowers Everywhere

"Think of your child, then, not as dead, but as living; not as a flower that has withered, but as one that is transplanted, and touched by a Divine hand, is blooming in richer colors and sweeter shades than those of earth."
—Richard Hooker

All bereaved parents will tell you that they miss their child terribly and that they know that no matter how much time passes, this missing will never go away. The most common words I hear from parents is, "If only I could have my child back with me to hold and to love." I call this step "Wildflowers Everywhere" because it introduces us parents to practices that invite magic and wonder to bloom in our lives as we begin to connect with our child. This makes us feel a little lighter, a little more hopeful because not all is lost — after all, we are learning beautiful ways to keep our connection with our child alive!

Unless you have lost a child, you can't even begin to understand the magnitude of the void left in your heart. There is a huge crater in one's heart that will never ever be filled — it's true. However, one of the things I learned early on in my journey of grief was that my child was determined to let me know that he was around and he still loved me. Because I'm a skeptical person, it took large gestures and signs on his part for me to recognize something truly magical was happening and feel his presence around me. But what he did was so loving that it changed my life and my grief forever.

I want to share with you what began to happen at around three weeks after Christopher's death. First, he began to appear in my dreams, vivid dreams that felt like visits during which he would hug me tightly and tell me he loved me. Then, a few weeks later, as I have already described in Chapter Four, when I was absentmindedly browsing at a Hallmark store, I felt suddenly drawn to a music box that happened to play "our song" — a coincidence that gave me the definite sense that Christopher had *chosen* it for me as his gift for me that Christmas — my first one without him. About a week later, on Christmas morning, I was awoken by the sound of running steps going rapidly down the stairs and stopping by the

Christmas tree. Both of my other children were in bed, along with the dog, our only pet, so this sound would have been an utter mystery, had I not immediately felt an inner knowledge that it was in fact Christopher. The steps went up and down and up and down again loudly, so that I would have no doubt whatsoever as to what I was hearing. Christopher had always *loved* Christmas — what child doesn't? — and that year, we had purchased the largest, live, pine tree we had ever gotten so I think it must have pleased him very much. I only wished I would have thought of buying him a symbolic Christmas present. All of these signs happened within a month of his passing, and it did not end there. Anyways, as I continued to struggle with the lows of grief, he continued to visit me in dreams, which made me feel reassured and loved when I was at my lowest. Another thing that began to happen was that if I was feeling very sad, I would notice a cardinal or a monarch butterfly — the kinds of birds and butterflies he particularly loved. They would show up and linger around me to make sure I had gotten the message that Christopher was still around me, loving me. I cannot begin to express just how helpful it was for me to receive these messages. He also had made a large collection of feathers, which were dear to his heart, and I found that, at times when I was feeling very sad, feathers would appear out of nowhere to offer me support and love. It has been twenty-one years now since his death and I still receive his messages of love and reassurance through signs such as these. My children actually helped me realize that Christopher was leaving messages for us. My son Jonathan would point to the fact that the street lights would flicker off and on at times and would tell me he knew his brother was letting him know that he was around, and my daughter Elise would let me know that Christopher was tickling her. So in a way, they were the catalysts for my realization that he was communicating his love to us.

The reason I am sharing this with you is that I want to help you keep the special and unique connection you have with your child alive. The death of my son opened a door for me to the spiritual side of things, and for that, I am deeply grateful. Please understand if I could have him back by my side, I would gladly go back to having that door closed, but since I have no control over these things, I can tell you in that connection to the spiritual and magic side of life, I have found a never-ending spring of healing and hope.

I know I am not alone in having these experiences. Many parents I have helped in their journey of grief have recounted for me the ways in which their child has sent them messages to keep their connection alive. Here are some ways you can invite your child to connect with you:

A Letter to Your Child

I think the best way to start is to go to a quiet place where you know you will not be disrupted. With pen and paper in hand, begin to write a letter from your heart to the heart of your child. Ask them to give you clear signs so you can understand they are still around. Explain to your child just how much you miss them and ask your child to put a healing balm on your heart and fill it with peace and love because you are having a very difficult time and need so very much to keep your connection to them alive. Write anything else you need and keep that letter to read aloud whenever you need to feel close to your child.

Spirit Whispers

What are spirit whispers? This is the way I like to call the seemingly random ideas that pop in my head, fragments of conversations I hear from strangers that somehow resonate with me, books that seem to jump off the shelves which seem to tell me I need to read them, or words that stand out on the television screen. Before my son's death, I had been closed off to this kind of guidance from God, the angels, etc. They probably had sent me an innumerable amount of messages and clues that were totally lost on me. Why was that? Because society at large does not seem to provide us with this sort of education, or it makes us feel like we're crazy if we believe in intangible signs and connections, so we end up doubting ourselves at times. What a pity this is, truly, because as human beings we experience so much anxiety and fear, which could be diminished and helped by knowing how to connect to the guidance, support and love available to all of us — if we know where to look and ask for it.

One major thing that happened to me after Christopher's death was that a lot of fears left me. For example, I am no longer afraid of flying in airplanes or of dying. If the plane goes down, I will be reunited with my son and that would make me happy. The fears I had about my other children — something bad happening to them — also left me because I had realized I did not have any control over whether they got sick like Christopher or not. All I could do was to ask for their protection, take the measures I had at hand to make sure they were well-taken care of and then let it go. Releasing those fears went a long way in helping me heal, but what was most helpful was the newfound awareness I had of the spiritual, unseen realm from which my son could communicate with me and to which I could ask for help, healing and peace.

We human beings often neglect the fact that when we focus our attention on something, powerful and transformative things can take place. So as soon as I focused my attention on any little sign from my son, I became attuned to words, writings, animals, smells, sounds, songs, etc. that resonated within me. These things I was drawn to were invariably the exact message or sign I had needed in that moment to help comfort or inspire me to have better thoughts, feelings and a wider perspective. What do I mean when I say that these things "resonated" with me? What I mean is that they stayed with me; they seemed to be calling me; their energy was reaching out for me. Have you ever passed a book at a bookstore and felt like it was calling your name, only to find it was the exact book you needed at that time? Have you ever walked through a store and heard a song playing in the speakers overhead, which you hadn't heard in years but which holds a memory that made you smile? When you begin to live from such a place, where you notice these kinds of things and are grateful for them as signs sent to you, then you are listening to your intuition and trusting that the messages you are receiving are guiding you in life toward a beautiful, new phase of growth.

Signs and Messages

When our child is trying to communicate with us, the signs and symbols they use to do so are such that the parents and/or siblings can recognize them right away as unique and clearly connected to their child/brother or sister. In my case, cardinals — his favorite bird — and monarch butterflies still show up in my life when I am in most need. I have a photo of him at a butterfly garden with a monarch sitting on the palm of his hand. Seeing these animals were clearly messages from him, as were the feathers appearing out of nowhere.

The timing was important because those messages did not happen randomly; they happened at the times when I *most* needed a hug, a loving nudge and they inevitably helped me feel better. Can you think of the things your child most loved? Having those in mind will help keep you attuned to any signs from him or her.

Children can also use music to communicate to you that they are around you. I vividly remember driving to my son's gravesite on the first anniversary of his death — my two children sitting in the backseat — and reaching to turn the radio on only to find myself so surprised and so in awe of the fact that our song, "Somewhere Out There," was playing at that exact moment! What a crystal clear sign of his presence; it brought such peace to my heart that he was there with us and that he was letting us know that he loved us. Is there a special song that connects you with your child? If so, you can ask your child to use that song to communicate that they are still with you and then keep your ears open to noticing the signs!

Angels

I don't know if you believe in angels or not. People always tell bereaved parents that now you have an angel in heaven — and there is nothing wrong with believing or thinking that. For me, I never thought of Christopher as being an angel, the kind you see in statues and paintings; what I did think was he was now in spirit form in a realm that is invisible and yet real, just like love. I realized, as a spirit, Christopher could still love me because love never dies, and I could still love him even though I could not see or touch him anymore. Since a new door to the spiritual world opened up for me with his death, I also felt nudged toward connecting with the angels. I bought a deck of Angel cards and used them as I asked for guidance in my life and struggled with how to live again without my beloved child. I am now on my third deck, and they help me by providing me with guidance as I try to navigate the difficulties that come with life. I have to say I am grateful for the fact that I now have the awareness of many loving presences in unseen realms, just waiting for us to ask for their help; we don't have to go at it alone because help, support and love are just around the corner — invisible yet as real as you or me.

Your Child and Their Magic

The most commonly known meaning of the word magic is as a noun, the power of apparently influencing the course of events by using mysterious or supernatural forces. This is not the kind I am talking about. What I am talking about is magic as an adjective: meaning wonderful and exciting. So when I refer to the magic of life or the magic of your child in this section, rest assured I am not imagining a rabbit in a hat or any sort of illusions or tricks at all. In fact, real magic — the wonderful and exciting one — is what exists *beyond* the illusion of normal societal constructs. Your child who has died is now dwelling in that magical, invisible realm at the heart of life and which you are connecting to whenever you feel pure love. They can be your bridge to connecting with it because the love that they gave you while alive was magic in and of itself, and it continues after death. Let me give you an example of this magic in action:

Before Christopher's death, I felt I had to solve all the problems in my life without any outside help, which made me feel alone in many respects. I had forgotten God is available to help and so are the angels. I had forgotten that these invisible forces could put people and circumstances in my path to help me in life. I was floundering. I felt trapped in an unhappy marriage and could see no way out. However, seeing my son's wise, old-soul eyes as he sat in the car behind me on our trips to the hospital, watching his calm acceptance of death and the purity of his love for me opened me up to the magic that exists in life even before he died. In the months before his passing, it was as if he already had one foot in another dimension, and it opened me up to realizing I did not need to go through all this alone, so I began to ask for guidance and help from the angels and God, and I received it at every step of the way. After my son passed, his love permeated through so many signs he sent me, and it was like he had led me through that open door so I could truly understand the fact that we are never alone, and there is help from invisible realms guiding us along in our lives.

My grief for my son will never go away; it will always be there as a perceptible and weighty pebble in my heart, but that loving and magical connection that continues and will be there until I take my last breath and possibly beyond that will always exist. It was by allowing Christopher to teach me from beyond the visible realm that I have been able to remain open to all kinds of other signs and affirmations from him and the universe, which have helped me take steps toward further happiness and letting wonderful things bloom into my life like wildflowers, things such as writing this book!

With his persistent efforts to connect with me, my son ushered a new way for me to look at life in a magical way! I began to notice things I had never noticed before, like synchronicities. What are these? They are defined as the simultaneous occurrence of events that appear significantly related but have no discernible causal connection. This is something that happened very often to me and to one of the mothers I helped.

Maria

A mother whose daughter had recently died, Maria was devastated and felt destroyed from the inside out. She did not know how she was going to go on. One day she decided to visit her daughter's gravesite, and on the way, she thought hard about what she could get to adorn it. She got there and continued pondering, "What would my daughter like to have around her stone?" While doing so, a large rabbit suddenly appeared out of nowhere (I have mentioned this story in another chapter, but I am adding to it now.), and she somehow knew deep in her heart that this was a message from her daughter that she was with her at that moment. Still in awe about the event, Maria felt the need to go to a home and garden store to pick out some flowers to plant around the grave, and as she was gathering different flowering plants, she came across a small statue of a little girl holding a bunny in her hands and knew that her daughter was letting her know, was actually picking out for her what she wanted to have around her grave. So she bought the statue and placed it on her grave while feeling touched by what had happened.

This series of events — the appearance of a rabbit at Marguerite's daughter's grave and her coming across the statue together with her desire to find something that would please her daughter — is a synchronicity, pure and astounding. When this sort of thing happens, you know deep inside of you that it was not a coincidence. It is important to trust your gut feelings or instincts because they are always right. They constitute the infallible compass we can use to guide us in life and will not lead us astray. I know this now, but long ago, I disregarded my gut feelings all the time and allowed my fearful mind to rule me. I am so glad that is no longer the case!

How about you? Have you experienced synchronicities and received signs that your child is trying to communicate with you? And since your loss, do you think you have learned to trust in your intuition more than before your loss? What about the word magic? Does it resonate with you or perhaps not? Do you feel that it goes against your religious beliefs? Hopefully you can see that the magic which I write about here is in fact something innate to you, as we all were children once and lived from a place of pure, magical wonder. Have you noticed how children stop and marvel about things that adults would usually pass by, such as glittering little rocks, colorful leaves, the sounds birds make, the different shapes of clouds, etc.? That is because children are in touch with the magic in life, that sense of wonder most adults seem to have lost and which can add so much to their lives if only they were open to it. Are you open to welcoming this sense of wonder filled with seemingly magical signs, guidance, communications from your child and amazing synchronicities? If you haven't done so, I invite you to begin now. Trust me, it will change how you experience your life forever and for the better! It may have been a long time since you noticed the wildflowers blooming, but it is at the core of your existence from back when you were just a little child in a big world. Keeping your connection with your child who died alive, can help you see that they are truly everywhere!

Selene Negrette

Chapter 10 – Monarch Butterflies

"They put on quite a show as they turn their wings into the sun, then they quietly lift and they glide and they shift, so their butterfly life has begun."

— Julie Simpson

In my own personal experience as well as my professional experience, I have found that the struggle we bereaved parents encounter in our journey of grief is that our hearts are so seemingly irreparably broken that we cannot imagine how we can continue to live. In many ways, we do not want to continue. It feels incredibly cruel to us that the world just goes on as if nothing happened when we are feeling so broken and sad.

The only way I was able to live again was to learn to lean on my child Christopher. It was only through his determination to let me know that he was around me and through my desire to keep that connection alive that I was able to take the steps needed for my eventual healing and transformation to take place. I call this step the "Monarch Butterflies" step because they did show up in my life as a sign from Christopher that he was around me but also because butterflies are a symbol of new birth and new beginnings. We could say that after the loss of our child, life as we knew it is gone, and a new phase, an entirely new life begins.

One of the things I often hear about from bereaved parents is that they go to visit psychics, mediums or angel communicators. I have done that as well, and I have to say that the experiences I had were incredibly affirming to me of their gift and of the fact that these people were simply conduits through which my child could communicate to me out of his desire to help me, out of his love for me.

I have also had parents tell me what happened during their sessions with mediums and how much their hearts were touched by the messages of reassurance and love they received from their child. Some of these parents had never before gone to see a medium and in fact were skeptical and thought they were all quacks; however, after their child's death, at some level,

they realized that maybe, just maybe it was possi⊦
wanted to communicate with them and they were ⌐.
up to that possibility. While speaking with a medium or oⅈⅈ.
spirit communicator can be a very powerful tool to help you
communicate with your child, the truth is, you already have
everything you need inside of yourself, to be able to be your own
conduit and receive messages from your child through your
intuition. Your child can be your most helpful guide in helping
you figure out how to live again. The love your child has for you
is unconditional and so immense that they are determined to
help you for as long as it takes because your child wants only
what is best for you; your child does not want you to suffer
forever; your child knows that as a parent your pain is deep, but
they also know if you allow love to guide you, you can learn how
to live again. Your child understands the pain you feel at not
being able to touch, care for or love on them, but what your child
needs you to get in touch with and know deep in your heart is
that they are still around you, loving and helping you. Your child
wants you to open yourself up to their help. I am including here
a link to a powerful meditation I have created for you, to help
you connect with your child. Click or go to the link below, and
download the meditation onto your computer or other device,
so that later on, at a time of your wishing, you can listen to it
through headphones and be guided on a visit with your child.

www.notyourusualgriefbook.com/ch10-guided-meditations

Visiting With Your Child: A Meditation

A good way to facilitate your communication with your child is to go to a quiet place, shut out the world for fifteen minutes or so, put on headphones, empty your mind of any thoughts as you enter a relaxed state and close your eyes. Begin to imagine your child in front of you in your mind's eye. The two of you are on a beautiful, rolling meadow filled with flowers of all colors: yellow, orange, white, purple, pink and blue. You feel the sun on your skin and see your child radiating a beautiful pink and purple light. Their eyes convey to you so much love that you feel a warmth envelop your heart's area, and this warmth feels very healing to you. You look into your child's eyes and after a little while, begin to pour out your feelings, your worries and your fears. Do not omit anything. Let it all out. When you are done, gently ask if your child has a message for you, a message to help you deal with everything you are facing. Ask them to give you a sign you would know without a doubt that it came from them to let you know you are on the right path. You look into your child's eyes and feel so comforted and so at peace because this feels like a visit, and it is wonderful to be in your child's presence again and feel all the love. You thank your child with all your heart for having come into your life and for continuing to be here for you, even after death. You let them know you'll love them forever. Finally, you ask your child to come nearer so that you can hug and kiss them, and you actually feel their arms encircling you.

This does so much good to your heart because you have missed this so very much. You tell your child so long until the next time and wave as your child walks away and disappears in the horizon. Open your eyes slowly and write down anything you think is of importance.

Affirmations

Are you familiar with affirmations? I had not heard about them until my son was diagnosed and my mother gave me the book "You Can Heal Your Life" by Louise Hay. Affirmations are positive statements you create and repeat to yourself, which reinforce the reality which you want to be living in. For instance, do you find yourself constantly worried about money and wishing this were not the case? An affirmation such as "I have more than enough money for all my needs" would be a short and positive statement you could repeat to yourself whenever you find you are overwhelmed by your financial concerns. In reading Louise Hay's book, I became aware of the kind of thoughts swirling in my mind, thoughts full of fear, worry, sometimes anger, other times pain. What she helped me see was, I was bombarding my mind with negative thoughts, which were affecting my reality, my experience. I was constantly feeling exhausted and depressed, and even though I had every reason to feel that way, considering that my precious son was gravely ill and I was not getting enough sleep, I was making matters worse by holding those kind of thoughts. I realized I could change my reality by consciously working on holding more positive thoughts. The truth of the matter is, I was not successful in doing that while my son was alive; however, after his death, when I was down in the dumps and felt that I could not go on, I began with renewed focus to work on my thoughts. I had recently divorced my husband of fourteen years, Christopher had died, I was grieving and I had two young children — who were also grieving — to take care of. I was facing an enormous amount of fear, worry and stress, but I have to share with you that as I began to consciously hold more positive thoughts and turn them into affirmations by repeating them in my head every time I found myself having a negative or fearful thought, I started to feel more at peace, less stressed and more capable of facing whatever the future held for me and my children. This is a very powerful practice, one you can do anywhere, at any time, and which is worth considering as you make a plan to learn to live again.

As Louise Hay says: "An affirmation opens the door. It's a beginning point on the path to change. In essence, you're saying to your subconscious mind: I am taking responsibility. I am aware that there is something I can do to change."

I encourage you to develop your own affirmations because you know best which words will be helpful to you. However, I have included some examples of affirmations:

"The bond between my child and me is eternal, and it survives death."

"I pay attention to the signs my child gives me and I feel his/her love every single day."

"I choose to be kind to myself because I know my intentions have always been good and loving."

"I forgive others easily and I feel lighter when I do that."

"My heart is full of gratitude for the ways in which the world supports me."

"I am able to trust in my intuition every step of the way."

"I appreciate how friends and family help me at this time."

"I matter and because I know this, I make time for my healing and self-care every day."

"I am open to recapturing the sense of wonder I had as a child."

In my own journey of grief, I have found that making time to do rituals that help me feel connected to Christopher, to God, the divine or a higher power have made a huge difference in my life. I encourage you to try coming up with your own rituals and affirmations to help you as you continue in your journey.

Developing Your Unique Plan

My recommendation to you is you set some time aside to spend on developing a detailed plan using the steps in this book to help you learn to live again. This plan needs to be flexible, and only you can develop it because you know what works best for you. I would stress the importance of including a morning and a bedtime ritual that incorporates the "Blessing Your Child" practice as well as using positive affirmations throughout the day to help you when you are holding negative, dark thoughts. Writing letters to release your feelings and having a place to keep positive memories, photos, mementos, etc. to lift you up when you need it can also be very helpful. I also suggest you include self-care rituals, such as a weekly mani, a monthly massage session or anything that would feel pampering and indulgent. You deserve it, don't you agree? You have been through one of the most harrowing experiences in life and have survived it. You more than deserve it!

You can also include using Angel cards or any type of healing cards as a way to connect with God's guidance and tune into your intuition. Something I have come to realize ir journey is that animals were a gateway to the divi... sometimes, they came into my path and I just knew that they had a message for me so I started to look up the meaning of that totem animal that had shown up and the message was always right on target for what I needed at that particular time. To this day, I am so grateful for all the messages I have received and continue to receive from animals!

The most healing of the practices in my "From Winter to Spring" program is when you are able to connect with your child and feel the reassurance and love in the messages, signs and symbols they send your way. In your child and in your keeping that connection alive lies the key to learning to live again.

Meeting Your Future Self

One of the tools I have found helpful to bereaved parents like us in clarifying what it is we wish for ourselves is to hold a meeting with our future self by using a meditation. I have created one for you that you can download onto your device by using the link below:

www.notyourusualgriefbook.com/ch10-guided-meditations

Prior to the meditation, take time aside to be by yourself, making sure there will be no interruptions, turn off your phone, put on earphones if necessary and settle yourself in a comfortable position in a quiet place. Close your eyes and in your mind's eye, see yourself walking on a path. The path goes straight out, and very far off in the distance, you see somebody else walking alone. You start to run to catch up with them, and when you do, to your surprise, you find yourself face to face with your own self. You look into the eyes of your future self and begin to connect. You notice how your future self is dressed, their facial expression; do you look stressed or relaxed? Feel free to ask any questions that come to your mind at this time. Afterward, ask your future self to help you, to provide guidance to you so you can learn to live again. Share with your future self any doubts, worries and/or fears you may have. Ask for assistance in filling your heart with trust, confidence and reassurance that you are not alone in your journey and that they will help you find your way. Make sure you express your gratitude to your future self for their messages and support, and say "so long" until you meet again. Open your eyes slowly and write down anything you feel is of importance to you.

Envisioning Your Future

Are you familiar with vision boards? They are powerful visualization tools that can help us focus our goals of transformation and growth and make them into reality.

Here's my invitation: Create a vision board for yourself, specifically for the future self you want to be in six months or a year's time. You can do this on your computer, beginning with a blank page document, and when finished, you can use it as your background or you can make a tangible one with construction paper.

To accomplish this, cut and paste the words you need to surround your mind with to better help you achieve how you want to feel at the end. Also look for photos of people, places or activities that resonate with how you want your life to feel and look like. Feel free to add anything you want as long as it is positive, inspiring and helpful. When you are done, place it somewhere you can see it often and make sure you take a small amount of time in the morning and bedtime to look at it while imagining all of the things you put on the vision board are already taking place. For instance, if you wish to feel peace, you might put the word "peace" or a picture of a tranquil nature scene on your vision board. When you gaze at it every morning or night, imagine you are already feeling peacefulness emanating from every cell in your body. Your life is full of peace, and you are feeling grateful from your very core.

Likewise, your vision board may also have more concrete goals: I could be your wish to have financial security so you might add an image of a pile of money or the words "financial security." The important thing is that every part of your vision board be something you truly wish to bring into your life.

Making this part of your morning and bedtime routine impresses upon your psyche that all of the things you put on the vision board are already taking place and will help it to come into being in the world because you are already feeling, at least for a portion of the day, that these things are a part of your reality.

By using all these tools, you are actively shaping your new life from the inside out, just like a butterfly who is still inside of the chrysalis, but is pushing her way out slowly but surely. Be patient with yourself and know that at the right time, you will be ready to emerge from your cocoon as a full-fledged monarch!

Chapter 11 – The Big Obstacle

"It is not as though I am averse to getting on. I only wonder how you can do it when your spirits are so weighed down you cannot move."

— Manju Kapur

Every individual grieves in his or her own way. As human beings we are all so unique in our ways of coping that it is hard to determine whether any particular program will be successful in helping a particular individual. Having said that, I have found that bereaved parents respond the best to any helpful suggestions that provide them with a clear understanding of their deep and unique grief, especially ones developed by someone who has personally suffered the loss of their child and has been able to move through their own grief in order to live again. This is what this program: "From Winter to Spring" offers you, and I know that it can help you, but only if you are committed to doing the work.

The big obstacle is the timing. When we are newly bereaved, there is a period of time, which varies from person to person, during which we need to wallow in our sorrow and to be in the depth of our despair. We, particularly mothers, need to feel it, need to cry it, need to succumb to it before we can do anything about it. So it is of extreme importance for the timing to be just right. I would say at around nine months after the death of your child would be an adequate time — only if you feel ready— for you to take baby steps toward the process of learning to live again even though you don't want to but only because you know you have to.

Whichever length of time has passed since your loss, I'm so glad you've given this book a chance, and I want you to know that further assistance is an arms' length away. This book is only the departure point of an eight-week program I have developed, which takes you along the journey from inner winter to spring, with much deeper detail and one-on-one guidance tailored specifically to your needs. In the next chapter I provide all of the information you need to get in touch with me and become part of this program, should you wish to continue on this journey with me!

Conclusion

"The day you come home from the funeral, the first time you put food into your mouth, that is the moment you have decided to live."

— Unknown

The writing of this book was born out of a pure desire to help parents such as yourself move through the very dark tunnel that grief is and learn how to live again with a huge chunk of your hearts missing. What appears to be an impossible and unsurmountable task, if taken baby step by baby step, can be accomplished. I know this because I did it, and it transformed me as a person and changed the way in which I now look at life and even death. In this book, I have outlined the program "From Winter to Spring," which will serve as a balm to your sore heart and bring — slowly but surely — a little ray of sunshine and hope to your life, one that has forever been changed and not by your own choosing, which makes it so much harder to accept. This is an eight-week program, which goes deeper than my book, and provides personalized one-on-one guidance through the steps this book presents. In my own life, by using the tools in this program, I literally went from feeling I was in the middle of the coldest blizzard and frozen almost to death, to feeling lighter in my heart because of knowing that my child's love survived his death and because of being in touch with all the signs and messages he left all over to let me know he was around. I wish the same for you!

The eight steps are not easy. They require you to commit to feeling better and to welcoming more peace into your life. They require you to do some inner work. Because of this, it is important for the timing to be right. The first few months of grieving are so very difficult because we are coming to terms with so many feelings, possibly disappointments, regrets, anger, etc., and we are mostly functioning on auto-pilot, numb to the world because we have to be in order to survive. However, after nine months or so — the time varies with each individual — there comes a point when you might feel the need to do something different because you have to DO something in order to continue living this life. And yes, it is difficult. It is so difficult! When you recognize this and realize you are willing to work to learn how to live again, then that is the time to begin following the steps of this program. It is not for the faint of heart, but I *know* that you are a strong person; in fact, you are a WARRIOR who has survived the worst imaginable loss, so I know that you can do this!

My wish for you is that you reach the point when you know in your heart that you deserve to feel better; that you can create a life in which you continue to nurture your relationship with your child; a life in which you are in touch with the sense of wonder you used to feel as a child; a life in which you find out what you can do with all you have learned from what you have been through; and finally, a life in which you feel fulfilled and renewed every day because you are able to feel the love of your child and notice the many ways in which they let you know they are with you.

My wish for you is that you are also able to learn how to help your other children — if you have them — keep the connection with their brother/sister alive by using the tools in the book; and that you are able to use the connecting tools I describe to help you grieve alongside with your husband/partner while respecting the individual way in which each of you needs to grieve. Above all, I wish that after reading this book, and following the steps, you will have a newfound feeling of peace and understanding as well as hope for a life in which you continue to grieve for as long as you live, but your grieving has been transformed because you have used it as fuel to help you create a meaningful and fulfilling life.

Finally, there is something I would like you to do for me. Would you please share your success with me? I would love to hear from you as to how reading this book and following the steps of my program are helping you. Please do so by sending me an email at SeleneNegretteAuthor@yahoo.com. In sharing your story, you will be helping other parents by providing encouragement and motivation for them to follow your lead.

If, on the other hand, you have read this book, followed the steps of the program and have realized you will be able to benefit and heal faster if you have my personalized support by signing up for the eight-week program I offer, then let's go ahead and schedule a strategy session to discuss where you are and how I can be of help to you. You can get started right here by filling out this form:

www.notyourusualgriefbook.com/program-sign-up

Visiting: www.notyourusualgriefbook.com

Or sending me an email if that's easier. I'm at SeleneNegretteAuthor@yahoo.com

I hope to hear from you, and perhaps work personally with you soon!

"From Winter to Spring"

Acknowledgments

This book would not have been written if a beautiful brown-skinned boy with sparkling green eyes and a contagious mischievousness had not been born from me and had not died at the tender age of eight. This wise child opened up my eyes to a much wider view of life and death and to what we are to do in this world. With his dying, but even more so, his living, he changed my life forever. As a result, my life took a different course that has allowed me to help parents going through their worst nightmare. Thank you Christopher for choosing me to be your mother!

I also have to thank my beloved children, Jonathan and Elise. You have taught me so much about loving unconditionally; you inspire me to be better and love better every single day. Thank you for your sweet love! Elise, I also want to thank you for your ever-present willingness to lend your skills as an artist to my projects and for all the technical support you have provided to me — with never a word of complaint. You are a blessing!

Linda Bender and Kathy Quinlan, your undying support of my endeavors keeps me moving forward every day. Thank you for your friendship and your belief in me.

My heart is also full of gratitude toward the animal world and all the loving and encouraging messages I received while writing this book: my thanks to the chipmunk (get ready for a big change), to the red fox (magic is afoot), to the monarch butterflies (new birth), to the cardinal (listen closely to your intuition), to the crow (magical help), to the vulture (time of transformation is approaching), to the duck (difficulties will be easily handled), to the robin (Believe in yourself as you move forward. Know that you are supported in all ways). Your presence and loving messages touch my heart every single day!

My gratitude as well to the Archangels, especially Archangel Michael, for your affirming and loving messages.

Last but not least, I would like to express my gratitude to Angela Lauria and her accomplished team whose very inspired and genius of a program, The Author Incubator, made it possible for me to write this book. Without your solid support, generous teachings and tough love, this would not have been possible. You have inspired me to fly. Thank you!

About the Author

Selene started her working life as a scientist with a degree in Biochemistry. After her first child was born, she decided to stay at home with an eye to returning to school later. However, the Universe intervened and after the diagnosis and subsequent death of her oldest child to leukemia, she wanted with all her heart to help families such as hers and decided to change her career path to Social Work. She received her Master's degree in 2000 and for the past seventeen years has helped countless of grieving parents and siblings with her message of hope in the midst of the greatest sadness of them all.

Selene has decided that all the valuable lessons she gathered from both her personal and professional experiences needed to be put into book form to broaden the reach of her message and bring solace to the hearts of many. She lives in Michigan with her daughter Elise and her beloved dachshund Snoopy.

Contact:

SeleneNegretteAuthor@yahoo.com

www.Facebook.com/SeleneAuthor

www.notyourusualgriefbook.com

Thank You!

Hello fellow bereaved parent,

Thank you so much for reading this book, which I wrote just for you. I want to give you something extra — a gift — to honor the hard work it is to try to learn to live again after such a tremendous loss.

Here's the link to a FREE two-video series that will provide you with additional insights and information.
www.notyourusualgriefbook.com/Free-2-video-series

If you are ready to do this and would like to register for my program, you can sign up right now by filling out this form:
www.notyourusualgriefbook.com/program-sign-up
or by sending me an email me at SeleneNegretteAuthor @yahoo.com, and we can begin this journey together!

Made in the USA
Lexington, KY
15 April 2019